"To get noticed in today's marketplace you must overpromise and over-deliver. As MAACO moves to dominate the $9 billion cosmollision market, we have adopted *Overpromise and Overdeliver* as our internal slogan. This is a must read for anyone who wants to compete in today's crowded marketplace."

—Anthony A. Martino, founder, MAACO and AAMCO

"In-depth case studies, tremendous core insights—*Overpromise and Overdeliver* challenges even commodity businesses to find a bold new promise for their consumers!"

—John Striker, senior vice president, marketing,
Bumble Bee Seafoods, LLC

"In *Overpromise and Overdeliver,* Rick Barrera once again provides unique insight into how firms we all admire have succeeded in hyper-competitive markets. He explores how these companies have made big brand promises to their customers and then ensured that expectations were exceeded at every interaction. These firms understand that branding is much more than an ad campaign and have embraced the idea of fulfill-ing their brand promise as the key to their success. A compelling case for the importance of managing the right balance of Product, System, and Human TouchPoint interactions, *Overpromise and Overdeliver* is a road map for organizations seeking to establish successful brands."

—Chet Helck, president and chief operating officer,
Raymond James Financial

"*Overpromise and Overdeliver* is the most unconventional yet impactful approach to customer service and loyalty to ever hit the business market. This book will give you and the organization you work for a significant and unfair competitive advantage."

—Todd Duncan, *New York Times* bestselling author
of *Time Traps*

"Rick Barrera turns the theories of branding into actionable steps that deliver real value."

—Mike Lawrence, VP and general manager,
Insulation Systems, Johns Manville

"Rick Barrera provides fresh critical thinking on the important topics of brand building and customer service. A must read."

—Sandy Sanderson, executive vice president (retired),
Oracle Corporation

"In *Overpromise and Overdeliver*, Rick Barerra provides a fresh, dynamic approach to customer relationship management. He shows how to exceed customer and corporate expectations through unique Touch-Point Branding."

—Judith Dyar, director of customer care,
Continental Airlines

"*Overpromise and Overdeliver* is a wonderful reminder how we should all be looking at our businesses. There is much that all of us can take away from Rick Barrera's book that can help us all improve what we do."

—Sid Feltenstein, former chairman, CEO, and founder of
Yorkshire Global Restaurants

"Rick Barrera points to many companies that are wonderful exemplars of the Experience Economy—businesses that stage premier experiences precisely because they overpromise and then overdeliver! Those aspiring to do likewise should touch this dynamic book again and again."

—B. Joseph Pine II and James H. Gilmore, coauthors,
*The Experience Economy: Work Is Theatre & Every
Business a Stage*

OVERPROMISE
AND OVERDELIVER

RICK BARRERA

Overpromise
and Overdeliver

How to Design and Deliver
Extraordinary Customer Experiences

REVISED EDITION

PORTFOLIO

P O R T F O L I O
Published by the Penguin Group
Penguin Group (USA) Inc., 375 Hudson Street, New York, New York 10014, U.S.A.
Penguin Group (Canada), 90 Eglinton Avenue East, Suite 700, Toronto, Ontario,
Canada M4P 2Y3 (a division of Pearson Penguin Canada Inc.) · Penguin Books
Ltd, 80 Strand, London WC2R 0RL, England · Penguin Ireland, 25 St. Stephen's
Green, Dublin 2, Ireland (a division of Penguin Books Ltd) · Penguin Books Australia
Ltd, 250 Camberwell Road, Camberwell, Victoria 3124, Australia (a division of Pearson
Australia Group Pty Ltd) · Penguin Books India Pvt Ltd, 11 Community Centre,
Panchsheel Park, New Delhi—110 017, India · Penguin Group (NZ), 67 Apollo Drive,
Rosedale, North Shore 0632, New Zealand (a division of Pearson New Zealand Ltd) ·
Penguin Books (South Africa) (Pty) Ltd, 24 Sturdee Avenue,
Rosebank, Johannesburg 2196, South Africa

Penguin Books Ltd, Registered Offices:
80 Strand, London WC2R 0RL, England

This edition published in 2009 by Portfolio,
a member of Penguin Group (USA) Inc.

1   3   5   7   9   10   8   6   4   2

LIBRARY OF CONGRESS CATALOGING IN PUBLICATION DATA
Barrera, Rick.
Overpromise and overdeliver : how to design and deliver extraordinary
customer experiences / by Rick Barrera.—Rev. ed.
p. cm.
Includes bibliographical references and index.
ISBN 978-1-59184-268-2
1. Product management. 2. Brand loyalty. 3. Customer loyalty. I. Title.
HF5415.15.B37 2009
658.8'343—dc22
2008050019

Printed in the United States of America
Set in Warnock Pro
Designed by Amy Hill

While the author has made every effort to provide accurate telephone numbers and
Internet addresses at the time of publication, neither the publisher nor the author
assumes any responsibility for errors, or for changes that occur after publication.
Further, publisher does not have any control over and does not assume responsibility
for author or third-party Web sites or their content.

To my father, Enrique,
who had the principles of TouchPoint Branding
in his bones and taught them to me
in our family restaurant.
To my sons, Hunter and Dylan,
my perfect angel genius children, who have been
infinitely patient and understanding during
the process of writing this book.

CONTENTS

PART TWO: Overdeliver

OVERPROMISE
AND OVERDELIVER

Introduction

What if I told you that you could attract far more new customers to your product or service than you ever imagined? And also that you could do it much faster and for less money than you ever thought possible?

I know—it sounds too good to be true, a little like one of those infamous Nigerian Internet scams, perhaps? Well, you have every right to be suspicious in our fast-paced, cacophonous, no-holds-barred world. After all, you're really no different than your customers: They are suspicious, too, and that's why it's getting harder and harder for businesses to make solid connections with their customers that will allow them to build their brands into something that lasts through more than one product cycle.

But it doesn't have to be that way. Just look at Husqvarna, Patagonia, American Girl, and other breakthrough brands that you'll read about in the pages that follow. They have swept to the top of their fields in record time and stayed there. How did these brands so quickly achieve so much while leaving their competitors shaking their heads?

I've spent many years studying the strategies of companies like these, and I've pinpointed the secret of their success. It's a strategy that I call overpromise and overdeliver, and it offers a way to breach the barriers to uncommon achievement in today's crowded market.

The strategy begins with an overpromise, a specific and distinctive appeal to your customers. How do you develop that overpromise? In chapters 1, 2, and 3, I'll show you how to craft a compelling overpromise that speaks to the customers you wish to reach. And to widen your understanding, I'll relate the experiences of several successful companies that have outstanding overpromises.

By definition, an overpromise is a pledge to deliver a product or service that is radically different and has more relevance to your targeted customers than anything your rivals are touting. So when you follow up on your already world-beating proposition by also overdelivering on it, you further multiply the distance between you and them.

How do you go about overdelivering on your brand overpromise? The secret is to get all three of your customer contact points—product, system, and human, what I call TouchPoints—

aligned and focused on the goal of delivering extraordinary customer experiences.

I'll show you exactly how to make the most of your Touch-Points in chapters 5, 6, and 7 by highlighting the experiences of exemplary companies such as Yellow Freight, Progressive, and the Container Store, while also calling out the lessons they have to offer.

But to give you an idea of what I'm talking about, let's assume that your overpromise is all about ease of use. Your espresso maker, let's say, will do the job it is designed to do with no fuss or bother, without you having to resort to flipping through a manual, changing a brew setting, grinding beans, measuring and tamping the grind, and cleaning up spills and drips after the coffee is extracted. The Product TouchPoint that specifically delivers that overpromise is your prepackaged coffee pod. All a customer has to do is pop in the coffee packet, push the switch, and—presto—steaming espresso flows into the cup.

The espresso maker may be a huge hit with your customers, but if you want the kudos to keep on coming and your competitors to keep on lagging, you must align your System and Human Touch-Points to deliver the same level of great experience customers get from your Product TouchPoints. That means you must make sure that users of your machine can easily obtain the prepackaged coffee that supports the overpromise. If the packets must be ordered by phone or via the Internet (a System TouchPoint), you'd better see to it that the ordering system is accessible 24/7 and that it's fast, efficient, accurate, and easy to navigate. If you use live operators (a Human TouchPoint), they must be quick to answer a call, patient, pleasant, and well trained in taking mistake-free orders.

The first time a customer can't use your machine because an order of the prepackaged coffee packets is lost or delayed, your long-term success is endangered. Next thing you know, that espresso maker will end up on a basement shelf alongside a raft of other once-wonderful gadgets and appliances. In other words, if either your System or Human TouchPoints prevent you from overdelivering, your overpromise loses its punch.

Whether your company is big or small, the rules for overdelivering on your overpromise are the same: You must have an unwavering willingness to lift up your brand by polishing your TouchPoints to perfection and infusing them with the same surpassing qualities that define your overpromise.

In the pages ahead, you'll see that any organization, no matter its size or its mission, has the power to overpromise and overdeliver.

PART ONE

Overpromise

Welcome to Overpromise and Overdeliver, the approach that turns also-rans into winners, and it all starts with a compelling promise—indeed, an overpromise. This section shows you how to craft your own unique overpromise based on a complete understanding of your market.

CHAPTER 1

Overachievers Overpromise

H ard times provide an opportunity to create amazing successes. Despite all the talk today of industry consolidation, menacing imports, dwindling credit, inflation, stagflation, and shrinking margins, a few remarkable businesses have discovered how to win more and more customers. How? More to the point, how can you apply what they've learned to your company?

After studying these thriving enterprises, these contrarians, I've identified their key strength—a new approach to branding that beats the competition because it's infinitely faster and less expensive than any of the traditional methods. For reasons that will soon become clear, I call this approach overpromising and overdelivering. While reading the following cases, try to uncover what they have in common. (Just so you know, the answers will be provided before the chapter concludes.)

- **How do you turn a struggling start-up into a $100 million business in five years?**

The picture wasn't pretty. Robin Chase, chief executive officer and cofounder, had created a company providing a new twist on an old service. She had given it a snappy name, Zipcar, and established fleets in Boston, New York, and Washington, D.C. Her idea—to rent vehicles by the hour rather than the day—was gaining traction. But in 2003, four years after she began, Zipcar's board dismissed her. The company, awash in red ink, needed a new leader. Installed in her place was Scott Griffith. With a BS in engineering from Carnegie Mellon and an MBA from the University of Chicago, he had held posts with Boeing and Hughes Aircraft. More important, he had twice rescued stalled start-ups.

What Zipcar had done, Griffith acknowledged, was both impressive and appealing. It had placed dozens of vehicles in parking lots or gas stations in Boston, New York, and Washington, D.C., the three cities in which it operated. To reserve a car, members logged onto Zipcar.com, chose their pickup time and car model, then walked to the closest lot. A wave of their Zipcard across the windshield unlocked the car; the ignition key was inside. Then off they drove, with everything covered—including insurance and gas—by a low hourly fee and mileage charge.

If customers needed a car for just an hour or three—say, to go shopping or meet a client in the suburbs—Zipcar was more convenient and less expensive than its rivals Avis or Hertz. For many of its four thousand members, Zipcar made it possible to forgo car ownership entirely. Also, customers applauded the company-promoted, planet-friendly benefits of having fewer vehicles on the road.

The big question for Griffith: Was Zipcar scalable? He was a numbers man, a true believer in systems engineering and performance measurement. Before he could calculate how big Zipcar could grow, he would have to closely examine the fundamentals of the business: the demographics, the dollars and cents, the technology. In the end he concluded the opportunity was enormous: Zipcar could be a billion-dollar business, but only if big changes were made.

To begin, Griffith divided each city into zones instead of treating them as individual markets. Each had its own needs, its own personality, and he aimed to accommodate them. Once a zone was identified—Boston's Back Bay or Cambridge's Harvard Square, for example—and parking locations secured, he packed them with a dozen or so cars, up from the one or two vehicles per lot that had been the standard of previous years. That way, customers would find the specific model of car they ordered when they arrived. In an upscale residential zone, the Zipcars might be BMWs and used for weekend trips to second homes; near colleges would be Mini Coopers and Priuses, which were seldom driven outside the city. Marketing and advertising were narrowly focused on the individual zones with an effort to have Zipcar viewed as just another neighborhood business—"like the coffee shop or the dry cleaner," Griffith said.

Since Griffith's arrival, Zipcar has grown at an incredible pace: from 150 cars in three cities to 5,500 cars in fifty cities; from 4,000 members to 225,000; from revenues of $2 million to more than $100 million. And the company continues to grow at a double-digit rate each year. After all this, Zipcar has been in the black for four years.

That's a phenomenal achievement. But what was the key to Griffith's success?

● **How do you sell fourteen million dolls with a conspicuous lack of national advertising?**

Ask American Girl. This company was started as a small direct-mail business in Middleton, Wisconsin, in 1986. Today, sales of its dolls exceed all others except Barbie. Its first retail store near Chicago's Magnificent Mile grosses more than its mighty neighbors, including Ralph Lauren. And it has been joined by sister stores in Atlanta, Dallas, Los Angeles, and New

York, with Boston and Minneapolis set to open next. Some fifty million people receive company catalogs, fifty-one million more visit Americangirl.com, and, altogether, American Girl sales top $400 million annually. For girls ages seven to twelve and their families, the company has become an irresistible source of entertainment and education, a brand that has achieved nationwide notoriety and approval.

American Girl doesn't simply sell attractive eighteen-inch dolls. It offers the "whole world," as the company puts it, for each of its fictional characters: their clothing, furniture, all sorts of accessories, a series of books for each doll that tells her life story and recounts her adventures. The company also sells a selection of preteen clothes that match those worn by the characters. The Margaret "Kit" Kittredge doll, for example, is a nine-year-old from Cincinnati growing up during the Great Depression. Her books describe the hardships she and her friends endure, the courageous way they solve their problems, and how "Americans opened their hearts" to help one another survive those difficult times. Other dolls include Kaya, an eighteenth-century Native American, and Samantha, from the Victorian era. To sign up a child for the entire Samantha package—doll, books, furniture, and clothing—costs nearly $1,000. And if a girl wants her doll to have a new hairstyle? The price for this service at the Chicago store is a not-so-cheap $20.

Despite the expense, American Girl has sold more than 14

million dolls and in excess of 120 million books since it was started. And it has done so without offering the dolls at other retailers and with little advertising other than its catalog, which is sent out regularly to customers. How is that possible? Founder Pleasant Rowland tapped into a long ignored but obviously rich vein among preteen girls and their mothers by grounding the enterprise on the premise of wholesome innocence. A onetime teacher by training, Rowland was convinced that girls grow up too fast these days, that they need an antidote to poor female role models. She wanted her Pleasant Company and its dolls to teach and inspire, to impart both strength and resourcefulness through the dolls' stories, which Rowland calls "the heart of American Girl." (In 1998, Rowland sold her company to Mattel, the maker of Barbie. It operates as an independent subsidiary, although Rowland is no longer with the company.)

The books are carefully researched and elegantly written. The story of the doll Addy, for example, was authored by respected novelist Connie Porter. Set in 1864, it is the tale of an African-American girl who was born into slavery and later emancipated. From the beginning, the line struck a chord with its intended audience, and the marketing—almost entirely online, by catalog, and word of mouth—has been amazingly successful. In 2008 a new twist was added with the release of the independently produced film *Kit Kittredge: An American Girl*, starring the Academy Award–nominated actress Abigail Breslin. It earned $15 million in its first six weeks alone and introduced the brand to thousands of potential customers.

The retail stores have drawn more than twenty-three million visits from girls and their mothers from a host of countries around the world. All the stores are enormous, lavishly appointed, and beckoning "girl places," appealing to all ages. They feature attractively decorated restaurants offering classic teas and luncheons, comfortable restrooms, and sleek marble floors. Lush red velvet couches invite mothers and daughters to read a book or simply share a quiet moment.

Girls and their moms flock to the stores for "A Day at American Girl Place" that begins with cucumber sandwiches, cinnamon buns, and chocolate mousse. Next is a fashion show featuring preteen models. Then they go downstairs to the 150-seat theater for a musical production that includes both modern characters and figures from the historical dolls' stories. The performers sing and dance and highlight the American Girl themes of resourceful heroines behaving admirably in challenging situations. A girl and her mother can have these experiences—plus a CD of the songs, a doll T-shirt, and a $120 in-store credit—at a cost of $250.

Few stop there, however. One visitor from Wisconsin, her eight-year-old in tow at the Chicago store, bought two $99 dolls, several books about each, and an array of accessories. The bill added up to $650, more than twice what she had planned to spend. "It's a racket, but it's a good racket," she cheerfully told a

Forbes reporter. "The kids get strong historical role models and stories that teach them a lot about life. You actually feel good spending the money."

So of all these tactics, which is the real secret of American Girl's success?

- **How do you run a franchising business for forty years and keep outdoing yourself?**

Marianne Dalcero was close to crying. Richard Kerley tried to comfort her. "We're going to make this place safe and livable," he promised. Within a few days, Tropical Storm Fay had deposited more than two feet of rain on the town of Melbourne, Florida, and Dalcero's home was one of hundreds savaged by floodwaters. Kerley, owner of a Servpro Industries franchise in Miami, was directing a crew of a dozen men as they tore out rotting drywall and plugged in dehumidifiers. They had been at work for four days, logging shifts of twelve hours or more, cleaning and restoring homes all over town.

The time spent with people who had lost so much was nothing short of emotionally draining, Kerley said, adding, "I was about to cry myself yesterday." One older woman, whose belongings were destroyed, couldn't afford a cleanup, but he helped her without charge. "What are you going to do?" he asked. "You can't just leave her."

Franchising is big business in the United States, generating annual sales of more than a trillion dollars. But it's a tricky business too. Building and maintaining a string of independent operations is a tough challenge, as any of the thousands of people who have tried and failed at it over the years will testify. Finding the right individuals to buy a franchise and giving them the help they need to make a success of it is an ongoing struggle, particularly in a faltering economy. Yet that is precisely what Servpro (based in Gallatin, Tennessee) has accomplished, year after year, for four decades—all while racking up double-digit growth and signing up seventy-five to one hundred new franchises a year.

Richard Kerley's Miami operation is one of more than fourteen hundred Servpro franchises in forty-nine states. They offer clients, especially insurance companies, a variety of remediation services for damage caused by fire, smoke, soot, water, mold, and storms of every type. They also clean household items, from carpets and upholstery to drapes and blinds. What sets them apart from so many other franchisees is the quality and quantity of the support they receive from Servpro headquarters.

The company was founded in 1967 in Sacramento, California, when Ted and Doris Isaacson opened a painting business. Two years later, they switched to cleaning and restoration and started a franchising operation. Within a decade, they acquired the Bristol-Myers Domesticare Division, with its 175 franchises. And the count was up to 647 in 1988 when they moved to Gallatin, attracted by the town's location within six hundred miles of half of the U.S. population.

When the Isaacsons decided to retire in 1995, they were determined to keep the business in the family. They convinced their daughter, Sue Steen, to leave her post as a CPA with Coopers & Lybrand and become Servpro's chief executive. Two more Isaacsons are in the wings—Randall, the president, and Richard, the executive vice president.

What distinguishes Servpro is its stiff requirements for franchise buyers. Applicants must have a net worth of at least $100,000, lots of business experience, and proven marketing skills. No absentee owners are allowed; franchisees must be both owner and operator. And they must pay a fee of $39,000 plus an ongoing royalty of 3 to 10 percent.

Once accepted though, franchisees receive plenty of assistance and guidance. It starts with an in-depth two-and-a-half-week training program at Servpro headquarters. Facilities there include a classroom with computers, scanners, and printers for software instruction. A fully furnished two-story house, erected within the training center, is the site for lessons in water and fire estimating and damage restoration. Also part of the center: six two-room mock-ups, where further hands-on instruction is offered by the company's sixteen corporate trainers.

Next, franchisees receive a week of education at their own location, courtesy of sixty field teachers. They get familiar with their remediation equipment and the detailed, well-tested business plan Servpro provides. They are advised on how to create and manage a Web site, organize their grand opening, and otherwise market their services. Company experts evaluate the franchisees' initial work in the field. And every year, Servpro serves up a national convention for all involved. Among the presentations: courses in the latest cleaning and restoration techniques.

A major attraction for franchisees is the Servpro brand, with its nationally recognized slogan ("Like it never happened") and the lime green color of its equipment. And it's also helpful to know that you can call on other franchisees near you to help. For example, when fires destroyed forty-eight thousand acres in New Mexico, Servpro's Catastrophic Loss Division organized a concerted response. Thirty-five professionals from eleven franchises in the Southwest moved in to help the Los Alamos franchise owner cope with the cleanup of hundreds of damaged homes.

One result of Servpro's careful selection and training procedures: The average annual total of turnovers and closed franchises has been a low 5 percent. Another result: a raft of awards and honors. *Forbes* magazine, for example, has chosen the company as the top restoration franchise in the United States, and it has made the *Wall Street Journal*'s list of the twenty-five highest-performing franchises.

But among all its techniques, what is the key reason for Servpro's long-running triumph in this high-risk business?

Promises Made and Topped

Part of what makes companies like Zipcar, American Girl, Servpro, and the others you'll read about in the pages ahead so successful is their ability to craft unique, attention-grabbing promises that radically differentiate them from their competitors. These companies don't just promise, they overpromise—and they align key elements of their organizations to overdeliver. Zipcar offers to give people "wheels when you want them," and with less aggravation and expense than anyone else. American Girl promises dolls that enchant girls and teach them how to live a life of substance. Servpro makes sure that franchisees have the best training and overall preparation in the restoration field. And in a crowded business environment in which everyone seems to be shouting the same message simultaneously at peak volume, exciting, breakthrough overpromises like these are the best way to stand out from the crowd. Let me be perfectly clear on one point: Overpromising does not mean promising things you cannot deliver. That's lying. An overpromise must have two characteristics. First, it must be radically different from competitors' pledges. Second, it must be highly relevant to customers.

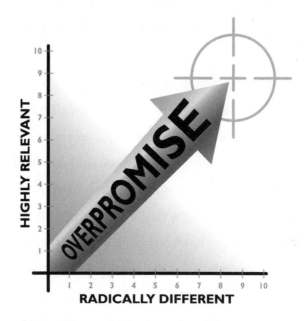

New companies must develop unique brand overpromises to battle their way into the marketplace. Established businesses, faced with fighting off upstarts and differentiating themselves from rivals, have to periodically overhaul (pun intended) their brand promises to adjust to changes in markets, competitors, and customers. After brand overpromises have been established, leaders must get their entire organizations aligned to deliver flawlessly on those promises and, above all, consistently every day with every sale or interaction.

Why? Because a promise is, by definition, a serious commitment—a pledge to do or deliver something by a particular time, without fail. Now, to overpromise may sound strange. After all, any business can promise the moon or anything else, but not just any business can deliver when it overpromises. Therein lies the advantage.

By overpromising, you put your whole reputation for honesty on the line. It says that you are confident your brand will perform at a level beyond your competitors', and you've made a solemn contract with hundreds or thousands or millions of customers. If even a few customers find you reneging, their contempt may well spread like a California wildfire. A wise leader knows that trust is the hard currency of business success. The price for squandering trust—sabotaging a brand's covenant with customers—is always too high to pay.

This book draws on case after case of unusually rapid success to show how to create and keep a brand overpromise. Just as important, if not more so, it will explain how masterful use of three distinct customer contact points—what I call Product TouchPoints, System TouchPoints, and Human TouchPoints— must be aligned in order to overdeliver on your overpromise and inspire unshakable customer loyalty.

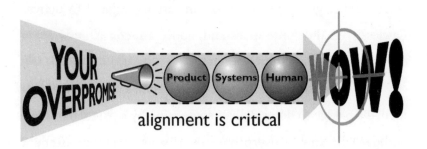

TouchPoints

- Product TouchPoints occur where customers interact with the product or service a company is selling. In other words, these TouchPoints describe contacts in which the customer actually experiences, handles, buys, uses, and disposes of a product or service, and they are the primary factors in most buying decisions. For Zipcar, a Product TouchPoint occurs every time a customer settles in behind the wheel. When a girl hugs her American Girl doll, reads its story in a book, or changes its clothes, Product TouchPoints are manifest. For Servpro, every service the company delivers to a franchisee—from spreadsheet instruction to a business plan—is a Product TouchPoint.

- It almost goes without saying that Product TouchPoints become less powerful as products and services become commoditized. When one airline's flight hardly differs from another's, or when two brands of detergent are virtually the same, the user's experience plays a small part in the decision about which one to buy. But if you're determined to avoid commoditization—and most of us are—Product Touch-Points are essential. Take a cue from the way Zipcar has aligned its Product TouchPoint with its overpromise; make sure the customer's experience is consistently problem-free and enjoyable. Or follow the lead of American Girl and its overpromise-TouchPoint alignment, and keep expanding the number of wholesome experiences your customer can have with a particular product or service. Or, like Servpro, constantly look for new ways to help franchisees make a success of their businesses.

- Human TouchPoints occur when the customer directly interacts with an organization's people. Most companies rely far too heavily on human interactions. I'm not in favor of eliminating them all, of course. They make it possible to deliver on overpromises in ways that only fellow humans are capable of—by empathizing with customers, clearing up misunderstandings, tailoring solutions to a customer's own circumstances, and so on. It is at the Human TouchPoint that frontline people bend, and sometimes break, the rules (but never the overpromise) in a customer-friendly fashion. The sales and service people at American Girl are the Human TouchPoints at their respective stores.

- When it comes to Human TouchPoints, Zipcar is different from the other companies in this chapter. In fact, it is close to my exemplar of a business that relies sparingly on Human TouchPoints in service of its overpromise. Some Zipcar members make their reservations by phone, and they will come into contact with employees if a car they've rented breaks down. And local managers may throw an occasional party for members. But otherwise, Zipcar's Human Touch-Points are for the most part nonexistent.

- At the other end of the spectrum are such organizations as the Ritz-Carlton hotel chain, based in Chevy Chase, Maryland, that have built their brands on their overpromising, overdelivering frontline employees. The overpromise at the Ritz, whose fifty-seven hotels and resorts span the globe, isn't clean sheets and a delicious breakfast (although it provides both), but rather its incredible standards of service. No staff member is allowed to say or even think "That's not my job," and the lowliest busboy is authorized to spend as much as $2,000 to solve a guest's problem. The hotel manager will pick up the phone if it rings three times unanswered. To bring its Human TouchPoint into alignment with its overpromise, the hotel chain spends about 10 percent of its payroll on training and education. That's four times the hotel industry average.

- Does this extreme attention to service pay off? Because the Ritz-Carlton is a subsidiary of Marriott International, a breakdown of revenue and earnings figures is not available.

However, it is known that the Ritz-Carlton is a two-time re-cipient of the Malcolm Baldrige National Quality Award and has been recognized for its sterling service by numerous hos-pitality industry and consumer organizations, including *Business Travel News* and J.D. Power & Associates.

- System TouchPoints include all other points of contact be-tween a company and its customers. They occur when cus-tomers encounter processes (return policies, for example, and frequent buyer programs) or systems (technological tools like ATMs and Web sites) that facilitate transactions and interactions. A System TouchPoint is in overpromise alignment when a Zipcar member makes her reservation on-line or waves her Zipcard over the windshield of the car she reserved. It is manifest when American Girl provides a menu of hairstyles for you and your doll, or when a customer shops for a doll on Americangirl.com, or still another when a girl visits a restaurant and finds a doll-sized seat (anything the customer gets to keep is a Product TouchPoint).

- Seattle-based Amazon.com, which racked up almost $15 bil-lion of revenue in 2007 and had net income of $476 million, is a prime example of a business whose online retailing sys-tems and processes are so intuitive and helpful (not to men-tion in line with its overpromise) that its customers seldom have any need for traditional customer service. They find what they need and order it, get progress reports by e-mail, pay online with their credit or debit cards, and get their goods by express shipment. It is here, by the way, in the promise of technology, that companies can make their biggest gains by overdelivering, by reducing the variables that hinder consistently excellent service.

All three TouchPoints must be in line with an organization's overpromise if it is to overdeliver, though to differing degrees. All three require a substantial and continuing investment of funds and managerial energy if they are to do their job properly. What counts is not the size of the organization, but willpower— the determination to take your company's brand to new heights by honing the TouchPoints needed to fulfill your brand's overpromise. I can't overemphasize how important the job is. It is pointless laboring to devise a unique overpromise only to underdeliver.

What's Next?

The overpromise of this book is both clear and powerful: It can enable you to build a brand far more efficiently and economically than traditional advertising-based marketing. How exactly do you go about it? It's all done with an over-the-top brand promise and Touch-Points—and creating both based on a thorough understanding of your market. The chapters ahead take a tour of overpromising and overdelivering, starting with the basic buildingblocks—brand and brand promise—and how you can turn them into overpromises.

CHAPTER 2

What's a Brand Overpromise?

W hen speaking to business audiences, which I do quite often, the first question is usually: "How do I get started implementing what you suggest?" The answer is always the same: Develop a brand overpromise.

I'm always surprised by how many of the companies represented in these audiences don't have articulated brand promises—much less overpromises—of any kind. Often the statements from those that do are so fuzzy as to be indistinguishable, not just from direct competitors, but also from promises made by thousands of enterprises in any and all markets. These self-deluders say that their promise is "world-class quality" or "guaranteed best service" or "a company you can trust." My unspoken reply is harsh: So what? In a world where winners shout distinctive overpromises, these misguided businesses whisper little and set themselves up to lose.

A generic promise has no meaning to the customer. It has to be specific, and outstanding; it needs to be an overpromise. First, discover who your potential customers really are. Second, tell them how your product or service is different and why they should buy it. Third, align your TouchPoints to do exactly what you promise: In other words, overdeliver—always.

How?

Brilliantly.

Your investors and employees deserve nothing less.

To grasp the true power of a brand overpromise, consider the story of HardiPlank, a market leader in the home-building trade. How the company's executives found the right overpromise by focusing on its end customers and then overdelivered at each critical selling stage is nothing short of a triumph.

The HardiPlank tale begins in the 1980s when James Hardie, an Australian building materials company, came up with a way to use fiber cement for house siding. It was a huge accomplishment: Fiber cement is less brittle than ordinary concrete and almost indestructible. Sheathed in HardiPlank fiber-cement siding, a house is impervious to fire, rain, snow, hail, salt air, and insects, including the always dreaded termites and carpenter ants. HardiPlank is guaranteed for fifty years against warping, buckling, swelling, splitting, delaminating, and rotting. It comes in various widths, shapes, and surface textures, including cedar, and, unlike vinyl siding, HardiPlank is available in twenty-six baked-on colors.

A sure-to-succeed product? Hardie thought so. In 1989, with great fanfare, the company launched HardiPlank in the North American market—to underwhelming results. Builders didn't want fiber-cement siding. They preferred vinyl because it was easy to install and was supposed to outlast wood. In reality, HardiPlank was much tougher than vinyl, but it was difficult to work with, destructive to power saws, and not forgiving when it came to contractors' framing errors.

Ironically, HardiPlank's competitors saw the virtues of fiber-cement siding and quickly introduced their own versions. But given the product's reputation, builders bold enough to use it demanded deep discounts. For nine dismal years, price-cutting was viewed as Hardie's only way to compete in North America.

The end seemed depressingly near in 1998 when Lewis Gries, then president of James Hardie USA, took the HardiPlank team back to square one. The flaw in Hardie's thinking, the group decided, was the notion that siding is siding—a product so dull that most homeowners couldn't care less about it. This assumption had led Hardie to focus its promise on builders rather than homeowners. But eventually Gries and his team discovered that homeowners actually do worry about which materials can best provide the safety, warmth, and security they want in their homes. They also hate the cost and hassle of maintaining traditional siding materials.

Armed with this knowledge, Gries and crew were able to create an overpromise radically different from anything the competition was offering, one that clearly set HardiPlank apart from its competitors. It was aimed specifically at end consumers, not at builders, and it stressed HardiPlank's psychological benefits, the reassurance that, in a stormy world, owners of HardiPlank-clad homes could curl up safely behind super-durable, weather-resistant siding guaranteed to last far longer than they were likely to own their houses. And to prove that Hardie was serious—the heart of its overpromise—the company guaranteed its siding for fifty years.

Shrewdly, Gries drove that overpromise into the minds of Hardie's end customers with a three-pronged approach: public relations (amplified by word of mouth), strategic product placement, and advertising. Aggressive PR got media attention: A national magazine could tell the company's story with far more credibility at far less cost than an advertisement could ever achieve. When the ads did appear, they served to reinforce the media message. Smart move.

With its new focus and new overpromise, the company soon won endorsements from leading consumer magazines and trade publications alike—free publicity from impeccable sources, what every savvy marketer seeks. *Builder* magazine named HardiPlank one of the twenty most innovative products introduced in the past two decades and proclaimed it the best exterior siding anyone had produced over the prior six years ending in 2003. *Midwest Living, Southern Living, Coastal Living,* and *Sunset* magazines, as well as the cable channel HGTV, all listed it as the "siding of choice." *Golf Course Living* hailed HardiPlank as the number one way to add value to a home.

To reach end users directly and make Hardiplank even more visible, the company persuaded developers to place its siding on model homes and display it at builder-design centers. Next, Hardie's salespeople reinforced the overpromise by promoting it at large home-building companies, where decision-makers had already seen HardiPlank's favorable press notices. Finally, the company ran ads in *Sunset* and other shelter magazines to sell homeowners on the irrefutable benefits of fiber-cement siding.

Hardie's end run around the builders was remarkably effective. Demand for HardiPlank soared, leaving builders scrambling for fiber-cement siding at the risk of losing lucrative contracts to competitors. And guess what? All their complaining about HardiPlank's alleged defects simply disappeared, like snow in April.

Today, HardiPlank is the top-selling siding in the United States. It already protects millions of homes in North America. Since 1998, sales have leaped by an average 30 percent annually;

production has nearly doubled every year since 2000. By making a strong, believable overpromise to homeowners, Hardie reincarnated HardiPlank as the third most recognized brand among all building materials.

What's more, the company has branched out into a whole host of new product categories. It's now the only fiber-cement business that provides "materials for a full-wrap house," including HardieShingleside, HardieTrim boards, and HardieSoffit panels and fascia.

An inspiring story? A legendary comeback? Of course. But hardly commonplace.

Back to Basics

How do you develop an overpromise for a business or brand? As with just about every successful venture in life, it has to start with the basics. In this case, that means truly understanding the meaning of "brand."

I like to ask people, "What is a brand?" The typical response is that it's a mark or logo that appears on everything a company produces. It's true that the term "branding" comes from the practice of searing livestock with the mark of a ranch to signify ownership. But these days, branding means much more than a way to prevent rustlers from riding off with your property.

The great adman David Ogilvy defined brand as "the intangible sum of a product's attributes: its name, packaging and price, its history, its reputation, and the way it's advertised." A brand may also denote the product's purchasing experience, financing, ease of use, after-sales support, warranty, and lasting value.

Brands carry emotional impact; they connect with a customer's identity and deep aspirations. They can speak to a buyer's personality, communicate his or her social status, and fulfill deep-seated emotional needs. In the end, your brand sets you apart from the competition by the values and attributes your customers believe a particular product or service possesses and conveys, including its origins and associations.

Brand isn't anything tangible. It isn't the logo on a product, a corporate slogan, or even the value you provide to your clients. Your brand exists only in the minds of your customers. It's shorthand for a host of qualities, features, benefits, beliefs, and business practices that the customer associates with a company, and that he or she is willing to pay to acquire.

Take the Apple brand, for instance. When I ask people what Apple means to them, they say things like "innovative," "expensive but worth the money," "latest features," "user-friendly," "intuitive interface designs," and "cool." Yet, when customers shop for a cell phone, they don't go into an AT&T store and say, "I'm looking for a high-quality, innovative, expensive-but-worth-the-money, cool, user-friendly cell phone with the latest features and an intuitive interface design." Instead, they use their shorthand; they say, "I want an iPhone."

So it follows that the only way you can know what your brand is, is to ask your customers. Whatever they tell you is what your brand really is. What you think it is doesn't matter. The only brand you can own and leverage is the one that exists in the minds of your customers.

What's in It for You?

Building the value of your brand is probably the single most important thing that can be done to build the value of your business. Legendary investor Warren Buffett—whose name, by the way, is one of America's most powerful brands—has often said that one quality he looks for in an investment is the strength of a company's brands.

What's a differentiated brand worth?

Let's look at the Orville Redenbacher popcorn brand, which has convinced customers that it's different from ordinary popcorn. The company began by developing a product that was truly unlike any other, a hybrid popcorn with kernels that actually popped 10 percent more than existing brands. Then Redenbacher built its brand around a simple overpromise, "It pops more," backed up by photos of a brimming bowl.

What does that "pops more" translate into in terms of dollars and cents? Huge premiums, that's what. Store-brand popcorn sells for five cents an ounce, whereas Orville Redenbacher in a jar goes for sixteen cents an ounce. That's a 300 percent premium.

Premium pricing by itself is huge, but combine it with high volume and you have the Holy Grail of a highly successful brand. It's tough to achieve but certainly not impossible. As names like Orville Redenbacher, Lexus, Apple, Coach, and Callaway Golf have shown, crafting the right brand overpromise and overdelivering on it thanks to the right alignment of TouchPoints can lead to near-legendary status as a company whose products are so coveted that its sales continue to grow even as the price climbs.

I've stressed the notion that your product must be significantly different from those of your competitors. It's also critical that the aspect on which that product or service differs must matter to the targeted potential customers. For example, an auto manufacturer produces engine coatings that are unquestionably superior to those of its competitors. But if customers don't care about the latest breakthrough in coatings, they won't choose that brand because of it.

Defining the Overpromise

A brand overpromise expresses all the things that set a brand apart from the competition, all the characteristics that make it distinctive. But some people confuse brand promises with vision and mission statements, when in actuality they have little in common.

Vision and mission statements are usually created for the benefit of employees, investors, and other stakeholders and are intended to define the organization's competitive space, purpose, and goals. A brand overpromise is specifically for customers and is built around a product or service. Vision and mission statements may resemble an overpromise in that they signal to customers how the organization will conduct itself, and that's certainly important. But this benefit is only incidental to the real purpose of the statement.

Furthermore, logos, icons, colors, or other graphic elements aren't an overpromise, even though they may play a part in conveying it. Such symbols are merely the shorthand reminders of the brand and the feelings that linger from customers' positive experiences with the organization and its products.

A true overpromise should describe what the product or service will do for your target audience, how it is different from competing offers, and why a potential customer should buy it. An effective overpromise sums up the essence of the brand. For example, James Hardie's overpromise reassures homeowners that their siding will keep them snug and secure for at least fifty years. Whether simple or profound, the overpromise must be so radically different from what everyone else in the market is promising that the customer hears you even though you aren't shouting. In other words, great overpromises cut through the chatter because they speak directly to customers about an issue that matters deeply to them.

An overpromise also goes far beyond the utilitarian value of a company's product or service and the general category it occupies. A car isn't just a means of transportation, and a Lexus isn't just a car: Its overpromise conveys style, safety, luxury, prestige, and the envy of neighbors. An Indian isn't just a motorcycle, but a way of life that evokes the freedom of the open road and a somewhat rebellious nature. Coca-Cola is more than a soft drink; it's an American icon—and to drink it is to be part of the American experience (which is also why Coca-Cola suffers when anti-American sentiment flares abroad). McDonald's is about food, speed, and consistency, of course, but also clean restrooms and a place where you can feed your kids inexpensively, get them a new toy, and let them play in Playland while you have a cup of coffee or a soft drink. Target's overpromise of "Design for All"—which informs all of its TouchPoints, from advertising to merchandising to store design—basically pledges to shoppers that being "cool" needn't break the bank.

Brands with Great Overpromise

Every successful overpromise is unique and must be understood on its own terms. It springs from a company's careful, top-to-bottom study of how customers experience its product or service, coupled with a concentrated effort to express the promise both explicitly and implicitly. It is understood by and delivered on by the whole organization. The following cases illustrate the key points.

Good, Better, Best Buy

The original overpromise of Best Buy, the national electronics retailer based in Richfield, Minnesota, was brilliantly conveyed in its name. But the promise was hard to keep in a market crowded with competitors, all of them offering much the same products at nearly identical prices. Then Best Buy recognized that any "best buy" in electronics should include high-quality computer service and repairs, something that retailers, including Best Buy itself, had ignored. In the real world, of course, service had long been the curse of any personal-computer user, who had to spend hours sorting through online help menus or waiting to talk to half-baked techies at overseas call centers.

Like its competitors, Best Buy had been shipping off personal computers in need of repair to regional repair centers, which meant long waits for already unhappy customers. But in 2002 the company added great service to its overpromise. Best Buy bought the Geek Squad, a Minneapolis-based computer repair business with sixty employees. Its founder, Robert Stephens, was assigned the task of transforming his squad into an army of electronics experts to be stationed at Best Buy stores across the country.

He did it, too. Today, thousands of Geek Squadders work out of more than thirteen hundred Best Buy outlets. They perform nearly half of all repairs in the stores. They also make house calls for a fee, traveling in Volkswagen Beetles. With its new brand overpromise, Best Buy offers customers something none of its competitors could match—the assurance that if anything breaks, Best Buy is there to fix it.

Even as Stephens was ramping up the Geek Squad, the company was testing another new twist for its overpromise. At the time, Best Buy stores were virtually identical, offering the same products in the same manner to whatever customers walked through the doors. Inspired by the work of Larry Selden, a Columbia University professor, the company studied the sales records of each store, pinpointing the most profitable group of customers. In a wide-ranging revolution—known internally as "centricity"—each store was overhauled to appeal to its particular golden customers—wealthy gadget lovers, middle-class soccer moms, and so on. At the same time, the company launched a massive training program to prepare salespeople to work with one or another of the customer groups.

So now Best Buy's overpromise includes another assurance: The best customers in any given store will receive special treatment in terms of the store environment, sales and repair assistance, and inventory. Good for them—and good for Best Buy. Even though the economy is down, the company reported an 11 percent increase in revenues and a 2 percent rise in earnings from 2007 to 2008. Overpromise, overachieve.

The Cool Mockery of Diesel

Selling clothing to young people is only incidentally about the clothes. Attitude and identity are what count most: sexiness for Calvin Klein; earnest social commitment for Benetton; hipness for Aeropostale. And for more than two decades, Diesel has prospered by poking fun at them all. The founder of this Italian company, Renzo Rosso, mocks the whole idea that a certain brand of laundry detergent, soda, clothing, or any other consumer product can make a person's life significantly better. His appeal is to an edgy generation of customers who know perfectly well how marketing works and who want to prove their savvy to anyone cool enough to get the message.

From its headquarters in the Veneto region of Italy, Diesel

will parody anyone—from Levi's cowboys to Benetton's social conscience. Models in one ad pout and preen like Calvin Klein's, all the while chanting ironically, "Thanks, Diesel, for making us so very beautiful."

In effect, Diesel's overpromise is a paradox: It offers customers a chance to prove themselves superior to the consumer culture. But paradoxical or not, it works. Diesel now sells in more than 80 countries and boasts 120 of its own stores, with an extended line of licensed goods and even its own hotel, the Pelican, in Miami Beach.

MinuteClinic's Debt to Jiffy Lube

One cold night in 1999, Jeff Krieger, a Minneapolis entrepreneur, rushed his son to an emergency care center, fearful that the boy might have a strep throat. They waited two long hours before their turn arrived. The test for strep throat was negative, and his son soon recovered, but Krieger never forgot the experience. The following year, it led him and some associates to create a company called QuickMedx. Its unique overpromise: to provide medical care for those common ailments that don't need the attention of a doctor or a hospital, and to do it safely, efficiently, inexpensively, and, above all, fast. Their tagline, "You're Sick. We're Quick," says it all—and each of MinuteClinic's TouchPoints is designed to make that tagline a reality.

On the face of it, the idea was as obvious as it was revolution-ary. Just as Jiffy Lube doesn't have to hire expert mechanics to complete an oil change, patients don't require physicians to treat an allergy or swimmer's ear, or to administer a vaccine.

QuickMedx set up small kiosks in local food stores and put nurse practitioners in charge. From the beginning, the opera-tion was opposed by the medical establishment, which in-sisted that it was dangerous for patients and an exercise in "discount medicine." The young company struggled finan-cially for two years before new investors eased out the found-ers and installed their own leadership team. The kiosks were sharply upgraded in terms of medical best practices, and the number of ailments treated was doubled. In effect, the initial overpromise was revised and expanded—and the company began to thrive. Along the way, the QuickMedx name was changed to MinuteClinic.

In 2005, a new chief executive with impressive marketing credentials further refined the company's overpromise. Nurse-practitioners were taught that their patients were also custom-ers. Complaints were embraced as opportunities to improve service. Nurses received sensitivity training that enabled them to better cope with emotional patients. The kiosks became friend-lier places.

One of the company's greatest admirers was CVS Caremark. In July 2006, sixty-six of the eighty-three existing Minute-

Clinics operated in CVS pharmacies. That's when CVS announced its acquisition of MinuteClinic. The sale price: $170 million. Two years later, in the summer of 2008, more than five hundred MinuteClinics were spread across the United States.

Promises Made, Promises Broken

Nothing kills a brand faster than an empty promise. Just ask Firestone, a unit of Japan's Bridgestone Corporation. It had thousands of tires recalled after tread separation was implicated in scores of auto-crash deaths. Besides the immediate costs of litigation and the millions of dollars in damages paid to victims, Firestone suffered incalculable harm when it lost the trust of customers. Efforts to repair the company's image continued when Bridgestone and its subsidiary Firestone made known its settlement of a nationwide class-action lawsuit, agreeing to spend more than $15 million on a three-year consumer safety education and awareness program.

Even a solid brand overpromise can come to grief when things go sour. In its early days, Intel leaped to the forefront of the microchip business with the tagline "Intel Delivers." The overpromise was great technology, world-class manufacturing, service second to none, and reliability. And Intel did overdeliver—until an unexpected uptick in demand coincided with a stutter in manufacturing. When CEO Andrew Grove's daily mail started to bring torn-out copies of Intel ads with the slogan altered to "Intel Never Delivers" or "Intel Delivers If You're Lucky," Grove called his agency and ordered the promise removed from all Intel ads.

Not a good idea. A brand exists in the collective mind of consumers, so it is tempting to use advertising, public relations, and spin to beef up the brand's image. You might try, for instance, to add value by making the brand seem youthful, cutting-edge, or otherwise appealing to your targeted consumers. But such tactics usually aren't wise, since, sooner or later, the customer's actual experience will have to live up to the image.

Smart business leaders craft their overpromise to emphasize the intrinsic value of their product or service, reinforcing the promise with the plain truth that the buyer will experience. For instance, Commerce Bancorp, based in Cherry Hill, New Jersey, promises to suit the customer's convenience instead of the bank's—and sure enough, its branches stay open into the evening, seven days a week.

What's Next?

You know what you have to do. That overpromise that was crafted so painstakingly only a few short years ago may by now have lost its punch with customers. A competitor, once eating dust, is now running neck and neck with you. Unless you're willing to be the one pictured in the rearview mirror, changes need to be made. But where to begin? First, reevaluate your current brand promise. The next chapter explains how to do just that.

CHAPTER 3

How Do You Build Your Overpromise?

So often in life, we're caught short by the abrupt transformation of someone or something familiar. A street where we go for haircuts, hardware, and housewares has become restaurant row while we weren't looking. It happens in business, too. Nothing lasts forever, including a brand promise, however successful it may have been. Changes in the marketplace, in your own shop, and in the tastes and circumstances of customers make it more than likely that your promise is no longer in sync with today's reality. A competitor has matched your quality, and customers have noticed. Or a target market has embraced a new set of priorities. For whatever reason, your current brand promise is not doing the job. You need something new, something tailored for a different environment—you need a new overpromise.

Where to begin? Start by evaluating and understanding your current brand promise. That's the only way it can be given the overhaul it needs. And that's where this chapter comes in. It brings order to the task of reexamining your product or service, particularly the elements that determine its advantages and disadvantages, and helps you use this new knowledge to update and electrify a fresh overpromise. It's critical, for example, to assess not just the end product or service, but also the consistency of all the operations, processes, systems, core competencies, and know-how, as well as the value of all trade secrets, databases, and proprietary software.

Eight Not-So-Simple Questions

Determining exactly where you stand now is hard work. A winning overpromise—whether it's brand-new or a rejuvenated version of a previous promise—isn't born of a sudden flash of inspiration. If it is to truly differentiate you, it must be built piece by piece. Attention must be paid not only to the intricacies of products and services, manufacturing and marketing, but to all the constituencies that must be on board to achieve a breakthrough. That means current and potential customers, employees, shareholders, distributors, and suppliers. After all, you will have to live with the overpromise for some time; align all TouchPoints with it; arrange the entire organization around it; and overdeliver on it. All stakeholders whose suggestions and support have an impact on your company's success must be part of the conversation.

To begin the journey to a complete understanding of your existing brand promise, consider the questions that follow. Also take note of the answers of a few companies that have demonstrated a knowledge of who they are, how they got where they are, and what their brands offer.

- **What is the essence of your business?**
  Why was the company started?
  What was the founder's vision?
  What did he or she plan to do better than anyone else?
  Are you fulfilling that vision now?

This first line of questioning is a way to get the coordinates, to zero in on the real reason so much of your life is being devoted to making the organization you work for work. A look at what was originally so exciting can also indicate whether you've wandered off course. Like a backwoods hiker, every so often you need to pause, look at your map, and check your compass. Otherwise, you risk getting lost.

Our first case study, the activewear company Patagonia, is an example of how an organization's essence can inform its over-promise—and how a company can retain a valid understanding of that promise even as the world changes.

Patagonia was founded a half-century ago by a young mountain climber, Yvon Chouinard, after he became disgusted with the quality of existing pitons, the metal stakes used to anchor climbing ropes. A blacksmith by trade, Chouinard hammered out a new kind of piton that was not only far stronger but reusable, which meant that mountains would not be festooned with rusting bits of metal. Chouinard's piton revolutionized climbing and eventually begat Patagonia, which, with its parent company Lost Arrow, went on to offer rugged clothing and accessories for lovers of all kinds of outdoor sports, from climbers to skiers to bikers. The company's overpromise: "We provide for environmentally responsible adventure."

In some ways, Patagonia's brand promise and its success evolved from a paradox: The founder's intense passion for mountain climbing and his great love of the outdoors led him to campaign for a scaled-down version of the sport—fewer climbs and climbers, simpler tactics, and less equipment. His goal was to preserve the vertical wilderness. Chouinard preached purity, simplicity, morality, responsibility, and restraint, hardly the watchwords of business and surely not a textbook case in the art of selling.

But what might seem like a wrongheaded approach to retailing proved to be the cornerstone of Patagonia's success. Serious climbers recognized that Chouinard's concerns were well-founded. Chouinard's insistence on high quality—"defects could threaten a life," notes Patagonia.com—coupled with his dedication to preserving the environment resonated with his target market. The company raked in $270 million in sales in 2007.

In the midst of what appeared to be resounding success, Yvon Chouinard decided to take stock. He ordered a review of the company's manufacturing operations, the aim being to gauge their impact on the earth. His conclusion: Patagonia had veered off course, losing sight of its environmental underpinnings. In short, the company's overpromise and the TouchPoints that overdeliver on it needed an overhaul. Determined to do what he could to protect the planet, Chouinard changed the materials used in the company's clothing, opting for organic cotton instead of the conventionally grown kind, which is drenched with dangerously toxic fertilizers and pesticides. Sure, the clothing would cost more, but he was adamant: "Now that we know [the environmental harm], it would be evil for us to do anything less."

A big part of the reason Chouinard's approach has worked so well is his constant efforts to know who his customers are, understand how they think, and make sure the company doesn't lose its relevance in a changing world. To do that, he keeps abreast of lifestyle and market trends as he refines new product ideas. What he knows for sure is that his customers are like him and in tune with the essence of Patagonia and its overpromise: passionate about the environment and eager to enjoy outdoor adventure, but always mindful of humankind's duty to protect the planet. As the company declares on Patagonia.com, "It is the style of the climb, not the attainment of the summit, which is the measure of personal success."

- **What are your brand's most important attributes? What do customers think of when they hear your company's name?**

Customers' interaction with a brand doesn't begin when they pick a product off the shelf. Their attitudes have been influenced by word of mouth, by advertising and public relations, by their feelings toward the store where they bought the product, or perhaps by a conversation with customer service personnel. Customers may feel strongly about matters you never even think of as being attributes of a brand. A company's decision to endure a strike rather than increase hourly wages, for example, or its sponsorship of a television show about breast cancer may lead some customers to express their feelings (positive or negative) with their pocketbooks.

My next case study, SmartPak, based in Plymouth, Massachusetts, knows precisely which one of its brand's attributes is most important to customers. That's because its founders' pursuit of the same attribute, reliability, is what led them to go into business in the first place.

Becky Minard started riding and caring for horses when she was ten and never stopped. By 1999, when this overpromise-overdeliver story properly begins, she and her husband, Paal Gisholt, had two daughters and a pair of Harvard MBAs between them. They both had held jobs as consultants, she in marketing, he in venture capital. In that year, Minard bought a horse named Westley, a beautiful, responsive animal that required special care—a joint supplement, vitamin E, and a 1,250-milligram daily dose of wormer.

Minard, who kept Westley at a boarding farm, assumed her horse was receiving the supplements he required. Then she realized the supply of vitamin E was lasting twice as long as it should, while the daily wormer was lasting half as long. A visit to the farm confirmed her worst fears: Westley was not receiving his supplements in the prescribed quantity.

Minard soon discovered that the problem was widespread among farms that board horses. When it was time to feed the animals, dozens of tubs containing powders or pellets had to be opened, the appropriate amount for one or another horse measured out, and the tub resealed. Often, in the hubbub, confusion reigned. The wrong animals received the wrong amounts of the wrong supplements. Container lids were left ajar or removed entirely, ruining the supplements inside.

These conditions had existed for generations, but Minard was determined to change them. Inspired by the divided containers that help humans keep track of their daily pill requirements, she designed a plastic strip of individual, easy-to-open wells, each labeled with the horse's name and holding a day's worth of supplements.

With her husband, Minard launched SmartPak in 2000, offering a very specific overpromise: They would provide for a horse's daily supplement dosage, and they would get it right every time. As a longtime horsewoman, Minard knew exactly how the owners felt about their animals, and she was determined not to disappoint them.

Inevitably, she occasionally fell short. Perfection is hard. But the founders came up with the perfect antidote: They established the tradition of the "failure to meet expectations" meeting. Customer confusion and complaints are faithfully entered into the IT system, and once a week the top people from around the company gather to go over every event in detail. In each case, they try to come up with a remedy that will keep the same problem from recurring—ideally an electronic remedy.

In fact, customer service in general is a major focus. Most orders are taken over the company's Web site, and a call center was set up to receive the others—and to handle whatever inquiries come along. Gisholt, the chief executive, and Minard, the senior vice president, staffed the center with equine experts, most of whom hold degrees in animal science. They routinely answer questions—from customers and noncustomers—about the best care and feeding of horses. Staffers are empowered to find a solution no matter how long it takes, with no one peering over their shoulders or timing their calls.

Another part of the SmartPak overpromise: The supplements will be provided to customers at a reasonable price. That would seem unlikely, given the customization of the product. But SmartPak has found ways to drive costs down. For example, the company sends out the packs on a monthly subscription basis for delivery largely through the so-called Barn Buddies program: By shipping several product orders on the same day to the same barn, everyone saves on delivery costs, and each customer can still pay by credit card.

The founders also worked with the supplement manufacturers. The steady, subscription basis of SmartPak deliveries, they pointed out, would enable manufacturers to better plan their production schedules and predict their cash flow. The manufacturers agreed and, as Gisholt put it, "shared some of those gains" with SmartPak, which in turn shared with its customers. As the company grew, its very volume assured manufacturer discounts. And then it brought out its own line of equine supplements, giving customers, in Gisholt's words, "cutting-edge formulas at factory-direct savings."

SmartPak today is a $42 million business, which has broadened to include dogs—supplements are delivered in smaller pouches instead of packs. But it has never lost its original focus on customer needs and on finding out about them from the customers themselves. It's part of the SmartPak brand overpromise.

- **Why do customers buy your product or service? Why don't they buy your competitors' product or service?**

If you think that asking customers why they buy from you will yield the same information as asking them to name your brand's most important features, you're wrong. People often buy for reasons unrelated to the attributes they cite. For example, I've used the same brand of toothpaste for years. I can list its positive features—it fights decay, whitens teeth, and tastes fresh, but that doesn't explain why I continue to buy it. The real reason is, my parents used it, and I've never felt the need to purchase another brand.

That said, however, I've also been shopping at the same supermarket for years, but I'm not all that happy with it. Checkout is slow, for one. I can also list some positive attributes—the people who work there are usually pleasant—but that doesn't explain why I continue to patronize the place. Simply put, I'm too busy or lazy to drive to a store located farther from my house.

Toothpaste makers may not be able to do much about my brand preference—it's emotional and too ingrained. Customers who buy a product because it reminds them of their childhood are a gift, something to be grateful for. But my food-shopping habits are another story; they could change immediately if a competitor built a new store nearby. By the same token, many a mediocre franchise or dealership that held on to customers because it was the only such operation in a particular area has been shocked to discover that customers bailed out to order from the parent company's Web site. Location can only carry you so far.

Asking customers why they buy from you can help to identify the kinds of people who are best served by your product or service. Chances are, they won't be the ones that were in mind when the brand promise was created.

Asking customers why they don't buy a competitors' products will bring a whole other set of revelations. To be sure, some of their reservations about your rivals will be predictable: The products are too expensive, poorly designed, or sometimes out of stock. But be prepared for explanations that have little or nothing to do with the rival products themselves. For example, a substantial group of customers may object to a leading competitor's reliance on overseas factories, where pay scales are below subsistence levels. Others might have read an article years earlier that accused your rival of fraud, or gender discrimination, or false advertising, and they have rejected its product or service ever since. Untold numbers of people still shy away from Chicken of the Sea tuna products, remembering a 1988 video that captured the sickening image of hundreds of dolphins dying in tuna nets. And then, of course, there will be those who don't buy another product because, well, they are simply in the habit of buying yours. Nothing about your brand promise or how it has been fulfilled has motivated them to look elsewhere; be grateful for that.

But with the new information gathered from the "why" questions, set about fine-tuning your brand promise to capture new customers and hold on to the ones you've got.

That's what Patagonia does with regularity. While its overpromise to provide for environmentally responsible adventure has powerful philosophical and emotional content, it also has a practical side, one that is grounded in Yvon Chouinard's personal insistence on moral restraint and responsibility. Consider Patagonia's guarantee of everything it makes. If you aren't "satisfied with one of our products at the time you receive it, or if one of our products does not perform to your satisfaction, return it to the store you bought it from or to Patagonia for a repair, replacement, or refund. Damage due to wear and tear will be repaired at a reasonable charge."

The company's design mandate, presented on Patagonia.com, also emphasizes its practicality: "Our definition of quality demands that any garment we make be long-lasting and strong. It should also be as light as possible for its intended uses . . . and easy to care for. It should be versatile and as unspecialized as possible." The products, like the overpromise, are constantly under review, as the Web site states, based upon "data from extensive lab and field tests as well as the experience of fellow employees and customers."

An example of Patagonia's close connection to its customers' interests and desires can be found at Water Girl USA, one of several separate divisions. As the promotional material illustrates, Patagonia knows exactly who inhabits its target audience. "When you're carving roundhouse cutbacks on your shortboard or throwing ends in your kayak," one piece declares, "you don't have time to fuss with 44 sport tops or shifting bikini bottoms." A few lines later: "We design our clothes to fit and flatter the muscular physiques of athletic women, with sophisticated styles and prints that won't make you look like a teeny bopper."

Many suggestions for product innovations and improvements come from employees, many of whom are outdoor athletes. But Patagonia never stops asking for its customers' views, and it takes them seriously.

- **Why don't noncustomers buy your product or service? Why do they buy your competitors'?**

Negative feedback can have positive results—if you're willing and able to put it to good use. Learning that some aspect of an overpromise, or of its supporting products and processes, is driving away a substantial number of potential customers should inspire some serious repair work. As Albert Einstein once observed, "We cannot solve problems with the same kind of thinking that created them. We must first identify failure, and then reverse it."

Sometimes, the problems noncustomers cite are all too real—a glitch in the product design, or maybe an irresponsible distributor. Correcting these sorts of problems may not be easy, but the sooner they are recognized, the sooner they can be corrected. Sometimes, though, potential customers stay away because of a misperception about a product, service, or organization, and that's a problem easily repaired with an overpromise. These noncustomers may have had a bad experience with a product years ago and, like those tuna boycotters, never realized that the problem has long since been fixed. Current customers apparently aren't bothered by such concerns, at least not enough to complain, so noncustomers are the only source for such negative information. Unless you talk to them, you'll never know what stands in the way of their becoming your customers.

Noncustomers are also well versed on the strength of competitors' brand promises and overpromises, information you need to set yourself apart. Asking noncustomers why they prefer another company's product will evoke a variety of responses, varying from the practical to the emotional, but they will help to discern the outline of a competitor's brand promise or overpromise. With that in hand, you can then craft your own overpromise.

That kind of differentiation wasn't originally part of the Pottery Barn brand promise. When the company first opened in 1949, the furniture business was dominated by big manufacturers like Ethan Allen and department stores were filled with conservative, affordable, nondescript chairs and sofas.

At first, Pottery Barn operated like many other furniture stores, buying its merchandise from old-line manufacturers and arranging it as a "collection." Eventually, though, perhaps after interviewing noncustomers, the company's leaders realized that middle-income Americans were interested in furniture with more flair and more personality than they could find in the traditional stores. Today, more than 95 percent of Pottery Barn's goods are exclusive, created in the company's design center across town from the headquarters of parent Williams-Sonoma in San Francisco.

Not listening carefully to what noncustomers had to say has left Starbucks with a bottomless cup of complaints and critics over what is perceived as feeble support for organic and Fair Trade products.

Seattle-based Starbucks made itself into a household name by spreading like a virus during the 1990s and early 2000s. By the spring of 2008, when its immune system collapsed and the effects of a too-rapid spread laid it low, the purveyor of pricey coffee drinks could count more than fifteen thousand company-owned and joint-venture licensed outlets in forty-four countries, including eleven thousand outlets in the United States. Soon, though, six hundred of its company-owned and forty-five of its licensed U.S. operations were waving goodbye to their last decaf, double tall, nonfat, extra-dry cappuccino-drinking customer. And thousands of Starbucks "partners" were looking for new employment.

Frequently lauded for its employee benefits—health care for both full- and part-time employees, stock options, a 401(k) retirement plan, tuition reimbursement, and more—Starbucks had positioned itself as a caring company, and the welfare of its suppliers and the health of the planet were part of its mission. But organizations that specialize in these causes, such as the Organic Consumers Organization (OCA) and the international human rights group Global Exchange, thought Starbucks was more talk than action. They believed the company wasn't living up to a promise made in 2000 to support the Fair Trade and organic-coffee initiative. The critics demanded that Starbucks increase its usage of certified beans to a "respectable level," which was somewhere well north of the 6 percent attributed to the chain.

Fresh from a winning battle to get Starbucks to stop using milk containing a cow growth hormone, the 850,000-member-strong OCA ramped up its effort to help coffee farmers by marshaling its forces to sign petitions and make telephone complaints to the Starbucks customer service line, while also encouraging people to buy their lattes and cappuccinos from presumably more farmer-friendly local, noncorporate coffee purveyors.

Starbucks continued to insist that it was an ethical and socially responsible company, trotting out facts and figures to support its claims. But the critics were not mollified, basically accusing the company of comparing apples to oranges by citing statistics of an "internal corporate responsibility model" that wasn't fair to farmers in the first place. While not necessarily a public relations disaster, the ongoing battle did nothing to help the company's battered image.

Having set itself up as a passionate defender of people and the planet, Starbucks couldn't afford to cut corners. When noncustomers point out discrepancies between what is being said and what is being done, it would be wise to pay attention.

Don't get me wrong. I still think Starbucks has done an

amazing job aligning its TouchPoints to deliver the perfect coffee experience for millions of people around the globe, but all companies, regardless of their current position, must listen carefully to their detractors.

● What emotions do customers feel when they buy and use your product?

Some products fail to evoke emotional reactions in those who buy them, but I have a hard time thinking of any. Even the humble paper clip can spur me to irritation if it's flimsy, or bring a smile if it comes in a bright color. We react to the objects in our lives on both an intellectual and an emotional level.

The products we use speak volumes about who we are. In our culture we are categorized and judged, at least in part, by the brands we display—the make and model of the car we drive, the restaurants we patronize, the watches we wear. Each purchase is, on some level, an occasion for deciding how we will be viewed by others.

What emotions does your current brand promise trigger? How do customers react when they see your product? Once again, the chances are good that you don't know as much about their reaction to your brand as you could. Over time, brand promises gather associations, negative as well as positive. When a company recalls a product because it is unsafe, or swallows another organization after a long, bitterly contested, and widely publicized battle, the events are incorporated into the brand. Even if you are aware of the troublesome overtones, you may not realize, unless you ask, how significant they are to your current—and possibly soon-to-be former—customers.

Pottery Barn's overpromise is more laden with emotion than most because it sells products for the home, a place that people care about deeply. Whether it's a tiny apartment in a big city or a rambling house in the suburbs, home is the one place in which we can create a safe, comfortable, welcoming, and aesthetically pleasing space. And most of us won't be satisfied unless that space meets two criteria: It must reflect our own taste, and it must meet with the approval of our family and guests.

By creating a lifestyle brand, Pottery Barn has found a way to meet both requirements. Its stores offer a mix of home furnishings and accessories ranging from chairs to wineglasses to candleholders, all bearing the mark of the same designers and all fitting into the same sophisticated style and atmosphere. The style is contemporary (but not experimental), and the quality is high. By any measure, the products are clean-lined and tasteful, and their sum—a lifestyle that has enormous appeal to a wide cross section of customers—is greater than their parts.

Pottery Barn's overpromise acknowledges that furnishing and decorating a home can be stressful by presenting the company as a kind of home decorating mentor. Salespeople are trained in helping customers mix and match the furniture and then add the appropriate accessories. The catalog offers plenty of advice, but Potterybarn.com's assistance is even more detailed.

At each point of contact, Pottery Barn pays attention to its customers' emotional needs. Their anxiety is soothed and their uncertainty resolved, so they leave the store, the catalog, or the Web site satisfied with the experience and pleased with the company that provided it. How does Pottery Barn achieve this virtual retailing nirvana? By paying attention to the emotional elements that play such a significant role in any overpromise.

SmartPak is no less concerned with its brand's emotional impact, as one might expect from a company born out of its cofounders' love of horses—and its overpromise speaks directly to its customers' identical feelings. SmartPak promises that their animals will receive the supplements needed for a long and healthy life.

In their communications with customers, in their catalog, and on Smartpakequine.com, the company's founders frequently recall their own well-earned credentials in most every part of the equine world, from hunting to dressage to trail riding. The message is clear: Not only are the founders knowledgeable about horses, but they also identify with their customers on an emotional level.

That message finds further expression in the call center where equestrian enthusiasts are invited to ask the experts on duty any and all questions concerning the health and treatment of their horses. That same approach can be found in a weekly blog on Smartpakequine.com called "Ask the Vet." Dr. Lydia F. Gray, SmartPak's medical director, offers the latest information on "What to Feed an Insulin-Resistant Pony" or "How to Slim Down an Overweight Horse." (The readers' comments, incidentally, give the company fresh insights into customers' areas of concern, information that can inform new Web site content as well as the product line.)

SmartPak sponsors all sorts of equine events, from races to festivals, as well as sharing its profits with horse protection organizations. Once again, the founders are saying to customers, "We understand how much you care about your horse's well-being. We know the feeling, and we want to help."

That's just one of the ways the company tries to stay in touch with customers to make sure they're getting the message and reacting with the kind of positive vibes SmartPak is seeking. Keeping tabs on the emotional response a product or service elicits is an important gauge for keeping an overpromise current.

- **If your brand was a person, how would you describe him or her? In the same vein, how would you describe each of your competitors?**

I'm not asking you to play The Newlywed Game, but rather to anthropomorphize. In ancient times, people attributed human characteristics to trees and animals, and we still ascribe human emotions to pets. Poets and playwrights find that anthropomorphization can free the mind to imagine the world (in this case, to imagine a brand promise and potential overpromise) from a new perspective, which is what makes the exercise potentially useful.

Try this: Compose a letter describing your brand as if it were a person. Is he or she young or old? Large or small? Mild-mannered or aggressive? Straightforward or shifty? Graceful or awkward?

Some other avenues to explore: How much schooling does your brand have? What kind of job? Single or married? How many kids? What kind of house? What kind of car? Favorite food? Sport? Movie? How does your brand dress? How does it spend its free time and with whom?

Finished? Now read over the letter. Think about the market in which you sell and your target customers. Would the person described in the letter be an appropriate salesperson for those customers? Would they buy from this person?

To get started, here's my image of the Pottery Barn brand as a woman: She's in her mid-forties, married, with a daughter in college. She manages a small department in a nearby department store and volunteers at her local no-kill animal shelter;

her husband sells insurance. Together, they earn enough to pay the mortgage on a nicely landscaped, three-bedroom home in a middle-class neighborhood, and to keep up payments on their two cars (hers is a Mini Cooper). She's an outgoing sort who's easy to talk to and is comfortable with who she is.

Next, perform the same exercise for each of your competitors. How do your competitors' brand people compare with your own? Who is best suited for the marketplace you share?

● How do your employees perceive your brand?

Every hour of every day, employees are deciding, consciously or unconsciously, how much extra effort to invest in their jobs. Nothing is more important to a company's success than convincing employees to invest more rather than less, because what you are after is their discretionary efforts on behalf of your brand.

Everything the company says and does—from community relations efforts to the quality of products and services—is part of the brand, and thus part of employees' brand experience. How they feel about that experience will largely decide how customers perceive the brand, so knowing where employees stand is crucial.

In the last few years, according to the consulting firm Towers Perrin, the boom-time tendency of many employees to focus on stock options and dreams of IPOs has been replaced by a greater concern for the soundness of a company and its treatment of people. Many organizations in turn have begun to recognize the need to mesh the way they treat employees with the way they present themselves to customers. The object: to earn the trust of employees as well as customers; to develop enduring relationships with both groups; and to deliver better on a new overpromise. The immediate benefits include reduced turnover rates, which eventually lower training costs and promote the consistency of employee performance.

American Express, for example, places major emphasis on employees' connection to the brand, to the degree that every employee's performance review includes an assessment by management of what he or she has done to support the brand.

At SmartPak, employee buy-in to the brand and its overpromise are among the founders' top goals. The chief means to that end? The company has gone to great pains to hire smart, imaginative, independent-minded people. It has provided extensive training. And it has then given employees their head. Errors of judgment are expected but repeats aren't acceptable, with new systems put in place to avoid such mistakes in the future. Since the beginning, according to Paal Gisholt, "we've placed tremendous importance on empowering individuals to make an impact while having fun along the way."

Determining how employees really feel about a company and

its brand can be difficult. In the case of SmartPak, though, the evidence is convincing. Gisholt was selected by Winning Workplaces, a nonprofit organization, as one of the eighteen "Top Bosses" in the country. The winners were chosen on the basis of employee satisfaction as well as such measures as benefits, investment in training, and the leader's personal vision. As it happens, SmartPak scores high in every category.

The company's incentives include employee stock ownership, open-book management, and a quarterly recognition program by and for employees. It also hosts a variety of company-sponsored social events and parties, many revolving around the employees' horses or dogs. (The percentage of staff owning one or both is extremely high—the population of the office virtually doubles on "Take Your Dog to Work Day.") Smartpackequine .com includes a blog by employees called "A Peek at the Pak," which is described as "our little place to blog, brag, play, pontificate, and share a little about our lives and the lives of our pets."

Along with Gisholt's emphasis on spotting and correcting failure, he and his colleagues are vocal about group and individual success. Whenever the company receives a complimentary e-mail from a customer, for example, a copy is sent to every employee. The object is to support and enhance a culture that thrives on hard work and accomplishment. As Gisholt says, "I have become a believer in letting our culture serve as the primary mechanism to generate alignment of goals within the organization, an 'Invisible Hand' of sorts."

Clearly, SmartPak's founders work hard to bring employees into sync with the company's brand overpromise, and they closely monitor the results. You would do well to do the same.

Putting It All Together

What do you do with all of the information you have gathered? Look for trends: What distinctions about your company are consistent across many or all of the stakeholder groups or questions? What common words do outsiders use to describe your company, products, services, or people? Examine the data for unusual phrases that may be the cornerstone for an overpromise. One of my clients recently found his company's overpromise articulated brilliantly by a customer, thanks to a brief telephone survey.

Here are the questions you really want the answers to: What is your reputation? What are you known for? What one thing about your company most matters to customers? Then build your new overpromise around it.

If you don't like the answers to these questions, you'll need to think deeply about what you want to be known for in the future and how your overpromise will articulate that clearly to customers and potential customers. You'll then be able to tackle the work of realigning each of your TouchPoints to overdeliver on your overpromise.

What's Next?

This chapter suggested how you can assess the intricacies of an operation to arrive at an accurate picture of the current brand promise and a clear sense of the attitudes customers and potential customers have toward an operation's product and its promise. Understanding your current situation is the first step toward crafting and maintaining a unique and powerful overpromise. The theory is, know where you are before making any decisions about where you want to go.

Now you're ready to take the next step. The following chapter offers some practical ways to get where you should be: firmly positioned to reap the rewards that come with a well-defined, tightly differentiated overpromise.

CHAPTER 4

How Do You Make Your Brand Overpromise Unique?

"What's missing?" is a question that's asked repeatedly at Husqvarna, the world's largest manufacturer of chainsaws, commercial lawn mowers, leaf blowers, and the like. The company, which is based in Sweden, is one of my clients. It is on a never-ending quest to fulfill its customers' needs even before the loggers, landscapers, arborists, and other professional users of its high-end equipment know exactly what those needs are. Employees of the North American operation, headquartered in Charlotte, North Carolina, regularly meet with customers on their own turf to learn how Husqvarna can better serve them. For Husqvarna, these efforts have paid off handsomely. Sales for 2007 were up more than 23 percent to almost $5 billion. Net income climbed too, to $300 million, an increase of 17 percent. Its gross margin was a hefty 29 percent, up from 27 percent the year before. Results like those make it clear that asking questions—and following through with imaginative solutions—is one great way to make your overpromise unique.

A few years ago, the answer to the "What's missing?" question turned out to be "profits" for landscape contractors. Landscapers constantly battle just to stay standing in the ring, and Mother Nature is one tough sparring partner. Too little rain and the grass doesn't grow enough to mow; too much rain and crews can't get onto the turf—until the rain stops, that is, at which point they can't mow fast enough to catch up. Early or late snow, or no snow at all, can be a blessing or a curse, depending on whether a landscaper also offers snow removal. Furthermore, the weather and the seasonality of the business heighten the challenge of recruiting, training, and scheduling crews. And, as if all that weren't enough, the high cost of workers' compensation insurance adds yet another burden, as does the constant strain of managing and maintaining the equipment needed to do myriad jobs.

Given the high rate of bankruptcy and turnover in the industry, it's no surprise that dealers who carried Husqvarna's products were facing similar profitability problems. Out of more than thirty-one thousand outdoor power equipment dealers a decade ago, only half are still in business today. The survivors lean heavily on manufacturers to finance their inventories, but shrinking industry margins threatened to put the squeeze on financing terms.

Enter Husqvarna. When the answer to the "What's missing" question came back "customer profitability," David Zerfoss, the company's North American president, and his team saw an opportunity. By changing their own strategy, they thought they could increase bottom-line results for both landscapers and dealers. Husqvarna began offering a product line that allows a landscaper to outfit his crews with equipment that shares the same controls and the same parts. The commonality means faster training of workers and technicians, quick interchangeability of engines and parts for on-site repairs, one-stop shopping for equipment and service, and one-vendor financing with Husqvarna's proprietary credit card purchase or leasing program.

Not only have cash flow and profitability improved for Husqvarna's landscaping customers, but its dealers are enjoying these rewards as well. Now dealers need only one line of equipment to satisfy customers, instead of the multiple lines they used to offer. And carrying a single line cuts costs, such as maintaining showroom and warehouse space, stocking inventory, and providing training for everything from repairs to sales to handling warranty claims. As one dealer near Husqvarna's

Charlotte headquarters explains, "I was always one bad season away from bankruptcy until I got with Husqvarna. Now I know I'm going to be profitable for the long haul. They've made this a viable business!"

And Dave Zerfoss says he's just getting started: "We've been methodically putting the pieces in place for several years." Husqvarna's success in the commercial sector has attracted "prosumers," he explained, defining them as consumers who want to use what the professionals use. "We are reinventing the industry for the twenty-first century," he concludes. "We are on a mission to change everyone's thinking."

Like Husqvarna, you too can come up with innovative ideas by looking at the world from customers' point of view. But that's not the only way to jump-start creativity.

Wiring Your Company for Bright Ideas

An overpromise is by definition unique, and that requires a bright idea—a differentiating characteristic. This might seem to contradict a point made in the previous chapter—that a successful overpromise isn't born of a sudden flash of inspiration. That's true, but the difference here is that the inspiration, the bright idea, won't really be sudden at all. It will be the product of your deepening understanding of overpromises and the work you do to find out what your customers really want.

To help you find your own spark plug, this chapter suggests areas to explore in the search for a potential new overpromise. In other words, it will prepare you to brainstorm the right bright idea. I encourage you to adopt a special attitude toward this task. Set aside the caution you apply when making decisions on weighty issues, such as the uncertain economy and weak consumer demand or your latest profit-and-loss statement. Sure, these are important, but in this case a more freewheeling approach is needed. The purpose of the exercise is to free your imagination.

Probe the gaps in customers' lives to uncover what they really want

Start by finding out what your customers need right now and what they think they will need in the future. Beware, though, the popular technique of simply gathering demographic data on customers. Demographic information goes stale quickly. Instead, delve deep into your customers' collective mind.

What you're looking for is information about people's lives and how they think their futures will unfold. The goal is to hypothesize about long-term trends, because it takes time—time to gather the resources necessary for developing the ideas, processes, and products that will comprise your new over-promise.

Here are some questions to ask current and potential customers: What are the three biggest challenges you face going forward? What's missing from your life right now? How do you think your life will change over the next five years? Ten years? What changes would you like to see? What one product would make your life easier or happier?

Answers to these questions will help you understand what people want in general, which is invaluable to discovering what they want in particular.

Some of the world's brightest business minds are attracted to the high-risk, glamorous fashion industry—and most of them end up burned. Millard S. "Mickey" Drexler became part of this group in 2002 when he was fired by The Gap, a company he had turned into a $14 billion American icon. But Mickey Drexler has since risen from the ashes. He has transformed a floundering, red-ink-stained J. Crew into a model of sales growth and profitability. It's the same trick he accomplished first with Ann Taylor, then with The Gap. How does he do it? By knowing what people want to wear before they do.

When Drexler arrived at J. Crew in 2003, the retailer, long known for its preppy clothes, was following the specialty shop crowd the way of Walmart—that is, down market. That seemed to make sense when the economy slowed and shoppers economized, but Drexler saw the situation differently. He would take J. Crew in the opposite direction. Customers of department stores and boutiques, he sensed, had soured on designer labels and designer prices. They were, as he told television talk show host Charlie Rose, "one market that's not being satisfied." Enter J. Crew with designer-quality goods but at affordable prices— a woman's blazer for, say, $350 instead of the $2,500 designer version.

Luxury for less—that was Drexler's overpromise for J. Crew, and it worked. The company had a successful initial public offering in 2006, just three years after his arrival. In 2007, he launched JCrew.com. As of the end of August 2008, he raised the number of shops to 195 retail and 61 outlet stores and boosted gross margins to nearly 42 percent, well above the industry average of 36.5 percent. Sales were up just shy of 16 percent—to over $100 billion—for the year ending February 28, 2008. Even as the company trudges through the current economic downturn, which Drexler describes as the worst retail environment he's ever seen, it is faring better than its rivals.

We can't all be Mickey Drexler, but we can learn from his example. Truth is, we've all gained knowledge and wisdom from our successes as well as our failures. And we've grown smarter by observing and being part of our industry's ups and downs. All that know-how is essential to the creation of a unique brand promise. The other major element is curiosity. Drexler is a store walker, constantly visiting his company's shops, studying what customers are wearing, which store's bag they're carrying, how they're reacting to the clothing.

For Mickey Drexler, an overpromise must be rooted in a clear sense of what customers want or are going to want. The way he finds out is by watching and listening. You could do the same.

Butt heads with conventional wisdom in search of overpromise opportunity

We all make assumptions, and we all adhere to a host of conventions. For example, we wait our turn in grocery checkout lines and don't raise our voices in movie theaters. In business, at least, all sorts of assumptions and conventions must be challenged and examined for opportunity.

Take the assumptions about how your industry operates. You and your competitors may agree on the standards that determine, say, a product's composition, price, or size. But each area represents a potential point of departure, an opportunity to develop an overpromise.

Consider digital books. For years, everyone in publishing took it for granted that they would remain a curiosity and appeal only to a small, tech-obsessed market. Then, in 2007, Amazon.com introduced the Kindle digital reader, which promises to do to bookselling what the iPod did to the music business.

Or consider banking. It has more than its share of engraved-in-stone, agreed-upon maxims, such as: Employees work short hours and never on Sunday, except for high-net-worth clients; customers will use ATM machines and the Internet, so branches can be closed and tellers let go; customers will tolerate long lines; and coins are to be shunned.

Commerce Bancorp, prior to becoming TD Bank, ran head-on into each assumption. Most Commerce branches were open from 7:30 a.m. to 8:00 p.m. on weekdays, but to accommodate early risers and people running late, the bank tacked on an extra ten minutes at each end. In addition, Commerce provided full-service banking for several hours on both Saturday and Sunday.

Tellers handed out lollipops to customers' children and dog biscuits to their pets. They took turns greeting customers as they entered. To prevent long lines at windows, Commerce cut the number of keystrokes needed for each routine operation: It took only twenty seconds to verify a signature and cash a check, for example.

Some banks either refuse to accept large quantities of coins or charge extra to count them, which especially irritates business customers making daily deposits. Commerce spent $10 million to develop and install Penny Arcades, machines that accept, sort, and count coins by the bucketful, then spool out a receipt for an amount that a teller either deposits directly into the customer's account or exchanges for bills.

Commerce Bancorp is a compelling case of a company that studied the unchallenged assumptions within its industry, and then crafted a winning overpromise by going against the grain.

But no matter what your business, finding a way to break with tradition could be your ticket to a breakaway brand overpromise. You and your colleagues may know everything there is to know about your company's product, but do you know all there is to know about its potential? Do you think about how it could be improved not just in small ways, like a bit more sand in the cement or a touch more red in the packaging, but through significant modifications that would create an overpromise? All around, in numerous companies and industries, managers are looking at familiar products through a new lens and suddenly seeing opportunities that no one noticed before.

Take Schindler Elevator, for instance, a Morristown, New Jersey–based division of Switzerland's Schindler Group. For years, the company made high-quality elevators that ran much like those of its rivals': Passengers pressed a button to summon an elevator, then another button to indicate their desired floor. The more people on the elevator, the more stops it made and the more impatient passengers (and people in the lobby) became.

The aggravation was even more pronounced in buildings with only one elevator bank.

Then Schindler employees challenged their product assumptions, which sparked a breakthrough idea: Passengers approaching a bank of new Schindler elevators see a central control panel on which to key in a floor number. The panel informs riders which elevator will carry them directly to their floor, after which it immediately returns to the lobby to pick up the next customer. This very efficient system moves more people in less time while demanding less space.

Another company that continuously examines its product assumptions is Progressive, an insurance holding company based just outside Cleveland, in Mayfield Village, Ohio. Progressive is discussed in more detail later in this book, but let me tell you a bit about this innovative insurer right now.

Auto insurance, including property-casualty and liability products, is Progressive's bread and butter. The company was founded in 1937 as a mutual insurer. Although it was innovative and successful from the start, it really became a contender in 1956, when it began to cover the high-risk clients that other insurers avoided. But even Progressive continued to reject one decidedly accident-prone group, motorcyclists—until, that is, its customer research turned up an interesting trend.

Although teenage thrill-seekers and macho high-speed rebels were still represented among motorcycle enthusiasts, Progressive found that a new and different group was growing rapidly. Middle-aged professionals—doctors, lawyers, businessmen—had taken up motorcycling. Many had joined touring groups, wheeling around the countryside on weekends, but for the most part their bikes spent more time in the garage gathering dust than on the road. Progressive decided to insure them. Today, it covers more motorcyclists than any other corporation, and it lays claim to being the only insurer endorsed by the American Motorcyclist Association.

One road to revising your product assumptions is to make a list of every problem reported by customers and then brainstorm solutions. Exclude nothing, even ideas that initially seem impossible. An "impossible" solution may inspire a workable one. Remember: Nothing about an existing product is sacrosanct; reconsider assumptions regularly. What you discover, and your ideas for improvement, could turn out to be a springboard to a powerful new overpromise.

Look past your current target market and focus on a new group if opportunity beckons

Companies that change course to pursue new target markets—and the new overpromises that they can spark—can achieve startling success. To be sure, a substantial part of the operation will have to change to accommodate the new market's demands, but if the result is a winning overpromise, and the winning business associated with it, won't it be worth the effort?

To spur inventive thinking about new markets, consider any customers whose attraction to the current product was a surprise, as well as those people whose interests you don't, and never tried to, understand. Then imagine what aspects of the product might prove valuable to each group and how they would use what is being offered.

Consider the example of defibrillator manufacturer Cardiac Science. After being spun off from Medstone International in 1991, the newly independent Cardiac Science focused on developing its automatic defibrillation device called Powerheart. All through their hospital stays, high-risk cardiac patients are hooked up to the Powerheart by electrodes. If a patient arrests, Powerheart automatically and instantaneously defibrillates the heart, starting it beating again.

Before Powerheart's introduction Cardiac Science suffered intense financial and technical difficulties. At the end of 1996 its entire staff consisted of two people. But then Raymond Cohen assumed the post of CEO and gradually got the company on its feet. In January 2000, Powerheart became the world's only automatic external defibrillator (AED) cleared by the U.S. Food and Drug Administration (FDA); thousands of them are now used in hospitals around the world.

Once Cardiac Science was on the right path, Cohen focused on broadening the company's overpromise to encompass a new market for portable equipment—a smaller, portable AED that could be used by police, fire, and ambulance services. As part of this initiative, in 2001 Cohen bought Survivalink, a competitor based in Minnetonka, Minnesota. The FDA cleared the marriage of Cardiac Science's software with Survivalink's AED hardware in February 2002. With the help of his purchase, Cohen had his new overpromise and a small and user-friendly product that has saved lives in locations as disparate as homes, schools, and amusement parks. Today, the company boasts customers in more than 160 countries and employs more than 550 people. And it has expanded beyond defibrillators to the development, manufacturing, and marketing of all sorts of diagnostic and therapeutic products in the cardiology field.

Rigorously review your business model

I'm continually surprised by companies that simply tweak their business models, rather than conduct a full-scale review. That's no way to accommodate the changes we are witnessing in business today. In one industry after another, new approaches are turning "business as usual" upside down. IBM chief executive Lew Gerstner, commenting on doing business in the twenty-first century, put it this way: "It's fun. It's a challenge, but if you pause, say goodbye."

No pausing here. Be the pioneer, break the new ground, reinvent your business model by linking it with a dramatically new overpromise. Of course, that requires fresh thinking and a willingness to embrace change.

Such thoughts must have come to the mind of Chris Jones, theater critic of the *Chicago Tribune*, when he sat down in June 2008 to review a new show. "In my fantasy world," he wrote, "I'd line up the managers of every business in America with lousy customer service and buy them all tickets to the Cirque du Soleil's 'Kooza.'" Once they were in their seats, he would ask them to behold "the rewards that flow from always exceeding your customers' expectations," rewards that weren't just financial but also soul-nourishing.

Make no mistake, Cirque du Soleil is a serious business. Its eighteen productions, two thousand products (from clothing to handicrafts), and restaurants and spas gross more than $700 million a year. And the incredible success of this brand has been built on a philosophy of never-ending change. "It's part of who we are," says Cirque's president, Daniel Lamarre. "Every time we come in a comfort zone, we will find a way to get out, because being comfortable in our business is very, very dangerous."

That sentence should be writ large on the portals of every business school. Being comfortable is very, very dangerous for any and every business. It means your guard is down—and an uncomfortable someone is gaining on you. It means you had better be developing a new and better overpromise.

Cirque started out as a touring group of jugglers, acrobats, and musicians in Quebec in 1980. One of its members, a fire breather and accordionist named Guy Laliberté, won a grant from the Canadian government to produce a show to mark the country's 450th anniversary. The 1984 performance, called Cirque du Soleil, or Circus of the Sun, had some of the major trappings of a circus, including wild costumes, acrobats, and original music. But no animals were to be found, and the intended audience was adults, not children. So Cirque avoided the huge expense of training and maintaining performing animals ("I'd rather feed three acrobats than one elephant," Laliberté likes to say), and it was able to set ticket prices much higher than for an audience of children.

The show was a great success, and Laliberté took it on the road. It gradually evolved into a clever, sometimes breathtaking blend of circus and theater, drawing on circus traditions from around the world, and at the same time introducing elements of character and plot. After years of financial ups and downs, Cirque landed in the center ring in Las Vegas. In 1993, its first permanent show opened to wild applause in Steve Wynn's Treasure Island hotel, and it's still going strong—along with four other Cirque shows in town.

The creation of a permanent Las Vegas show can set Cirque

back $200 million. *Wintuk,* a traveling act that celebrates winter, cost a mere $20 million to mount. Here's how it was described by the *New York Times:* "Computer-animated background screens, six 80-pound fluffy white puppet 'snow dogs,' a choir of swaying, singing 13-foot-tall lamp posts and menacing, 14-foot-tall ice giants. Aside from a backstage staff of 100, the cast of 48 includes 16 puppeteers, contortionists, teeterboarders, acrobats, jugglers, skateboarders and in-line skaters."

Yet in spite of the complexity and cost, Cirque produces a new show every year. And in spite of the huge success of its current offerings, that new show is always a major departure. *Kà* offered martial arts. *Zumanity* was part burlesque, part cabaret, and altogether sexy. *Love* was all about the Beatles.

Why does Laliberté insist upon taking that chance, year after year? For the same reason I urge you to constantly review your business model in search of a new and better overpromise. Change doesn't have to be revolution. It needs to take place within the larger mission of your company, in keeping with its personality and history and in line with your overpromise. That's a lesson Rick Alden took to heart when the amazing success of his start-up, Skullcandy, almost led him to forget where he came from.

A snowboarding fanatic with an entrepreneurial bent, Alden was a student at the University of Colorado business school in 1986, when snowboarding was just beginning to take hold. He and a friend created the first learn-to-snowboard demo tour—a pair of boards, boots, and lessons for $10 a day. It took off. Three years later, they were promoting snowboarding events and offering discounts on lift passes and the like through a membership card. Those programs were sold, and Alden used his share to produce the first step-in boot and binding system for snowboarding.

In 1999, flush with the proceeds from the sale of that company, Alden was riding a chairlift in Utah, music pounding out over his headset, when his cell phone rang. All was confusion for the next few seconds as he threw off gloves and headphones and went searching through his pockets for the phone. Why, he wondered, couldn't his headphone accommodate both music and phone calls?

In 2002, Alden came up with Link, a headphone that did just that, and his first pitch was, naturally, to those snowboarding shops that had bought his bindings. His new company, Skullcandy, was in no time turning out headphones designed for the snowboarder's taste ("They love a ton of bass," he says), followed by earbuds, hands-free devices, and MP3 players. In each case, as one innovation followed another, and one overpromise yielded to the next, Alden kept his focus on his core constituency, the cool young snowboarders, skateboarders, and inline skaters.

A turning point arrived when he sold Giro on putting Skullcandy speakers with Link in their snowboard helmets—and adding the words "Powered by Skullcandy" to the helmet packaging. After that, Alden said, his pass to success was in hand.

In 2007, he pitched Skullcandy to Best Buy, Target, and Circuit City, and to his surprise and delight, all three signed on to stock his product in all of their outlets. Suddenly his products were there among all the bicycles and sneakers and electric guitars for the whole world to buy—and the snowboard and skateboard shops represented only 10 percent of his revenue. The temptation was to switch his marketing focus to the mainstream, but Alden resisted. Skullcandy had to stay edgy and hold on to its core customer, he said, "because without him we'll lose people like me—old guys who want to buy cool young products." Today, 100 percent of the company's marketing dollars are spent on core customers.

Keeping up with—and ahead of—those fickle young customers is the task Alden embraced. They're as changeable as the weather over Park City, Utah, where Skullcandy is headquartered. But Alden is regularly revisiting his business model in light of those changes and altering his overpromise accordingly.

If your company isn't as proficient as Skullcandy at riding the big bumps of change, you, as the company's leader, must become its agent of change. Consider what weaknesses can either be strengthened or outsourced, and what strengths you can capitalize on. If, for example, your back-office operations are far better than those of your rivals, offer to become their back-office vendor. The bottom line: Regularly rethink every aspect of your business model.

Keep it simple, and watch a more substantial overpromise emerge

Whether changing a specific product, a marketing approach, or a supply chain, simplification can lead to a powerful overpromise.

Cleveland-based Sherwin-Williams did just that when it created a new plastic container for its Dutch Boy paint. The new container obliterated the inconvenience and aggravation of the old ones. How? With its twist-off lid and no-drip spout, the "Twist & Pour" simplified an unnecessarily messy and complex job. Customers couldn't get the improved product quickly enough.

Keeping things simple, whether it's a product or a business plan, means dispensing with distractions and confusions. It means getting to the point, focusing on what can deliver the best results.

Sometimes, as in the case of American Ecology, that process can take a while. But the Boise, Idaho–based waste processing company has finally moved beyond its longtime problems and gone on a tear. Since 2001, both sales and profits have shot up 400 percent, and the stock price has soared 1,000 percent. It was the culmination of a decision made a few years earlier to narrow the organization's focus and simplify its operations.

A company named "American Ecology" should rightfully be saving wetlands or lobbying for tougher pollution controls. Instead, it treats and disposes of hazardous, industrial, and low-level radioactive waste for both government and commercial customers, including steel mills, oil refineries, medical institutions, and nuclear power plants. The company's four treatment and disposal sites in Nevada, Idaho, and Texas handled more than a million tons of toxic waste in 2007, a 36 percent increase over a year earlier. "This business is pretty simple," Steve Romano, the chief executive, told *BusinessWeek*. "Once you cover your fixed costs, the profit is substantial." In 2007, the company boasted earnings of $19 million on sales of $126 million.

Up until now, the road was spattered with red ink and littered with brickbats. For fifteen years, ending in 1978, a predecessor company operated the Maxey Flats dump site in rural Kentucky. In 1984, that company joined with another waste disposal organization called Teledyne National to form American Ecology. The new venture was just beginning to see daylight when the Environmental Protection Agency informed American Ecology that it might be held responsible for the remediation of Maxey Flats, now designated a Superfund site because of the contamination of the area's groundwater. Newspaper accounts recalled an earlier claim that an American

Ecology dump had caused radioactive pollution of a lake in Illinois.

Despite all that, American Ecology prospered over the next decade. The demand for hazardous and radioactive waste disposal was rising rapidly, and the number of companies with experience in the field was limited. In 1993, the company went on an acquisition binge, acquiring several outfits that possessed waste processing credentials but also a variety of other interests, from solvent recycling to transportation.

In 1995, the roof fell in. Well-advanced plans for building waste disposal facilities in Nebraska and California crumbled. There were new charges of radioactive leaks from a company site. (California senator Barbara Boxer's widely quoted comment, "American Ecology's record is horrible," didn't help the company's reputation.) By year's end, the company had losses of almost $50 million on revenues of over $77 million, and the stock price was tanking. It hit $1.75 in May of the next year, down from $18 in 1992.

Wall Street was predicting the company's imminent demise, yet once again it rebounded. In large measure, that was the result of a decision to refocus American Ecology on its core services, the treatment and disposal of low-level radioactive waste and of other hazardous and toxic materials. Many of the acquisitions made just a few years before were sold off, and the cash infusion was used to buy businesses that supported the company's simpler overpromise. As chief executive, Steve Romano has maintained and extended this thrust toward simplification, and it has transformed once-struggling American Ecology into one of the nation's fastest-growing companies.

What's Next?

So you've answered all of the questions in Chapter 3, and done what I've suggested in this chapter. Now what? You and your team will need to sort through the data and articulate an overpromise around which your entire organization will align for the foreseeable future. The first step is to get it surrounded, by which I mean you should decide on your core attribute. What do you want to be known for? It may be speed, lowest cost, or a particular aspect of service that separates your company from all others.

Once you've got it surrounded, you must do the hard work of wordsmithing your overpromise. If you work hard enough, or are inspired enough, you will be rewarded with a timeless classic like M&M's "Melts in your mouth and not in your hands."

My personal favorite was the original overpromise for FedEx: "When it absolutely, positively has to be there overnight." No mincing words here. They made it absolutely, positively clear that they would get your package to its destination on time. And then they did it, time and time again, until they became the leader in overnight shipping.

Following the suggestions in this chapter will help you develop your overpromise. But a promise is nothing without a means of overdelivering it. The most efficient way to do that is to take full advantage of the three types of TouchPoints, the primary points of interaction between a company and its customers. Just ahead, in part 2, I begin with the Product TouchPoint.

PART TWO

Overdeliver

CHAPTER 5

How Do You Optimize Your Product Touchpoints?

T ime was when Yellow Freight didn't think much about its customers. Sure, it had plenty of them—some 300,000, in fact, who were paying the company $2.5 billion a year to haul heavy freight across the United States and, through a network of partners, around the world. But when customers called to arrange a shipment, no one asked when they wanted it delivered. Instead, they were given a delivery time that might or might not hold.

What mattered to the company at the time was efficiency. Employees tracked how much freight was moving, how much fuel was consumed, how full the trailers were packed. If a trailer was partially empty, a shipment was usually held until more goods were found and loaded. What customers wanted, the company believed, was low shipping rates. But with no measure of customer satisfaction, the people at Yellow Freight didn't really understand what truly mattered to those who hired them. When employees were asked how often goods were damaged, bills were wrong, or shipments picked up or delivered late, they guessed 10 to 20 percent of the time. In reality, the rate was 40 percent.

Customers finally got sick of the inflexible schedules and unreliable service. "Yellow was never willing to work with me," Timothy Slofkin, purchasing manager for Interprint, a printing company in Clearwater, Florida, complained to *Fast Company*. So he took Interprint's business elsewhere, as did many other customers. In 1995, Yellow Freight chalked up $30 million in losses and began its second round of layoffs in two years.

That's when Bill Zollars signed on as chief executive officer. His mandate: Rescue the company. His method: A new, customer-oriented overpromise. Yellow would give customers real-time control of their shipping with fast, cost-effective service from the initial call to final electronic payment for services. A twenty-four-year veteran of Eastman Kodak, Zollars had just built the Ryder System's integrated-logistics division into a $1.5 billion business. For him, the challenge of Yellow was irresistible. Over the next five years, he crafted and nourished a Product TouchPoint that put Yellow in tune with its customers, overdelivering on its new overpromise. His efforts were so successful that in 2003, Yellow acquired its largest competitor, Roadway, becoming Yellow Roadway (it has since become YRC Worldwide).

In the pages ahead, we'll catch up with Yellow and some other companies that have found impressive ways to improve their Product TouchPoints. First, though, let's revisit the concept of TouchPoints in general, what they are and aren't, and why they're so important.

TouchPoints are points of contact between you and your customer that help you overdeliver on your overpromise. I'm starting with Product TouchPoints because your product is what you sell. It's the reason you have customers in the first place.

As in the example of Yellow, Product TouchPoints are also Service TouchPoints, although I prefer to use the term Product TouchPoints to encompass both. A service, after all, is a product—a product of your company's ingenuity, its systems and processes, and especially of those employees who actually provide it. Most services today also include tangibles—a report of findings from a consulting firm, say, or an investment plan from a full-service broker, or a will from an attorney. But a few do not, such as a delivery service.

And Product TouchPoints include not only the actual product or service itself. TouchPoints also encompass product availability and ease of purchase. Is there parking near the store? Is the product in stock? In my size? In the color I want? Is the store open at times that are convenient for me? Is simple, one-click buying available if I want to order the product online? Product TouchPoints also cover information about the product, competitive offerings, packaging, shipping methods, financing options, warranties, parts-and-service availability, return policies, recyclability, and so on.

Even though Product TouchPoints are where your company's overpromise comes to life, disconnects between products and promises are all too familiar: stain removers that don't work; weight-loss diets that add pounds; magazine articles that fall short of their cover headlines; mobile phone service with spotty reception; toothpastes that don't whiten; gourmet restaurant meals that are anything but gourmet. The list goes on and on.

Some years ago, *USA Today* reported that one of every four purchases ends up being a problem for the customer. No surprise to me. I once spent an entire day trying to test drive a new car. Of the four dealerships in San Diego, where I live, two were closed, one was so busy that no one paid any attention to me, and at the fourth a salesman literally tossed some keys at me and said, "Have a good ride." Guess what? I bought another brand. The disparity between overpromise and TouchPoint was just too great.

Another reason why Product TouchPoints deserve special attention is that they get people talking—for better or worse. In fact, personal experience with a brand and word of mouth are what drive revenue growth today. Indeed, they are not only the top two reasons why customers choose a brand, but they are also an important marketing tool because they simply work faster, more effectively, and less expensively than any other approach.

Certainly, advertising has its uses, particularly in defending and reinforcing an already market-leading brand. And ads can absolutely be used as part of a strong mix of marketing methods. But relying solely (or even predominantly) on advertising to tell your story and differentiate your brand is folly. Today's customer has become, in whole or in part, pitch-proof.

What really does the job is buzz. And just how does the buzz get started? At Product TouchPoints, where customers get a chance to examine a product or service and react to it—and spread the word.

Now let's get started overdelivering on your overpromise with a look at how several winning companies have made the most of their Product TouchPoints. Each case highlights a number of ideas that might fit your own company's needs.

Let's begin by returning to Yellow. It represents a perfect alignment of Product TouchPoints with an overpromise.

The Yellow Way

When Bill Zollars assumed the helm of Yellow in 1995, he knew that a corporate culture that had evolved over seventy years could not be changed overnight. So he set out on an eighteen-month journey to convince twenty-five thousand employees to think differently. He began at 6:30 every weekday morning, speaking to the drivers at one of Yellow's more than 375 U.S. terminals. Then he talked to the dock crew, the office staff, and finally the sales force. At night, he got together with customers.

Zollars's simple but surprising message: Stop telling customers, "Sorry, we don't do that." The new message: "Yes, we can." Whatever the customer wants, the people at Yellow, he said, need to find a way to deliver it. It wasn't an easy sell, but these simple connections with often ignored but essential employees sent a signal that couldn't be ignored. In time, and with much repetition, the message sank in. "We've gone from being a company that thought it was in the trucking business to being one that realizes it's in the service business," Zollars told *Fast Company*.

Today, what that realization means for Yellow's customers is a shipping service designed to deliver a series of positive experiences. First, callers no longer encounter a one-size-fits-all long-haul carrier doing business by its own rigid rules. Clients now choose from a variety of services, including regional shipping and expedited shipping. Customized shipping is available for small and midsize businesses. Customers themselves decide when freight will be delivered—in a week, days, or even hours. They also specify morning or afternoon delivery, or in some cases, a specific time. And for expedited orders, Yellow offers a money-back guarantee.

When a repeat customer calls Yellow to do business, he discovers that the sales representative already knows where his company is located, what type of loading dock it has, the size, weight, contents, and destination of previous shipments, even who has signed for past deliveries. If the order is identical to a previous one—say, several thousand pounds of various-sized crates going from Chicago to Dallas—the customer can complete the process in about fifteen seconds.

Exact Express, Yellow's quickest, most expensive, and most profitable service, is also its fastest growing. One very tangible indication of how the Product TouchPoint is fulfilling Yellow's overpromise: Exact Express executes 98 percent of its expedited, time-definite, guaranteed deliveries perfectly. Most customers currently use the service mainly for emergency shipments, but the company sees it becoming a routine part of many just-in-time supply chains.

Company-wide, the defect rate has plunged from 40 percent to 5 percent, meaning that 99 percent of all shipments are flawless. Numbers like that go a long way toward changing negative attitudes. Revenues rebounded smartly to top $10 billion in 2007.

Yellow's transformed Product TouchPoint is supported by an impressive array of technology. The customer never physically encounters it and may not know it exists, but the technology—on which the company spends $80 million a year—helps its sales representatives, system operators, drivers, and freight handlers overdeliver by giving the clients what they want, when they want it, and making every interaction a pleasant one.

Take the profile that pops up on a sales representative's monitor when a customer calls. It's the product of a smart phone system that recognizes the caller's number and opens the file as the phone begins to ring. Out on the loading docks each employee is equipped with a wireless handheld computer that shows what is on board arriving trucks and where to put each crate. If unloading pallets takes longer than the system estimates it should, the computer alerts employees so corrective actions can be taken immediately.

The hub of the Yellow system is the central dispatch office at corporate headquarters in Overland Park, Kansas, a suburb of Kansas City. Like air traffic controllers, the dispatchers view the entire system and every truck in it on a huge electronic map of the United States. Every ten minutes the map updates itself and trucks on the road jump to a new location.

It gives dispatchers a high-level view of the day's shipping activity.

Each truck can be displayed with all the shipments it contains—color-coded to show whether they're on schedule—providing the data that enable customers to track their freight online, in real time. In addition, all the drivers in the system can be located and color-coded according to their availability. When the dispatchers spot looming service problems, they can work within the web of terminals and drivers to devise solutions.

Now let's consider some of the lessons found in Yellow's transformation of its Product TouchPoint:

1. Make it easy. The customer's convenience sometimes gets short shrift when TouchPoints are in the process of being honed. Not at Yellow. By making all of a customer's previous dealings instantly available to the sales representative who answers the call, a repeat order can be taken in a matter of seconds (variations take a little longer). Today's customers, be they businesses or individuals, have limited time and are under severe pressure to get a job done quickly. Speeding them along at the Product TouchPoint can keep them coming back.

2. Make it comfortable. Companies, like people, often feel more comfortable doing things themselves than

relying on suppliers. Why? It gives them a sense of control. Recognizing that concern, Yellow relieves the anxieties of customers by making it simple for them to track the progress of their shipments online. Product tracking may not apply to your business, but other ways of easing customer concerns, such as providing long-term warranties or money-back guarantees, can enhance your Product Touch-Point. Put your customer in control of your processes whenever you can. Where they can't actually be in control, give them as much information as possible.

3. Use technology in ways that truly matter to customers. Yellow has harnessed technology to deliver information to employees where and when they need it, not just at call centers but in behind-the-scenes operations. Truck drivers and dock employees are constantly informed about developments affecting their work, thus enabling them to adjust quickly if plans go awry. Getting the word out to your employees in real time can have an enormously positive impact on your Product TouchPoint.

Roger's Gardens—
Out of the Ordinary

Along a manicured avenue in Southern California's upscale Corona del Mar sits a seven-acre bit of horticultural heaven. It's called Roger's Gardens, and for more than three decades it has offered its discriminating customers the finest flowers and plants. The current version, though, is far different from what you might have found just a handful of years ago. That's because the owners took a hard-nosed look at their competitive circumstance and came up with a new overpromise—and a new Product TouchPoint to match.

In the past, like most garden centers around the country that found themselves in competition with Walmart, Lowe's, and the like, Roger's was watching as its customer count dwindled year after year. Weekend gardeners in search of a flat or two of petunias and pansies were deserting nurseries in favor of the low, low prices and convenience of the big-box stores. "We had our annuals in the same spot for 25 years," Gavin Herbert Jr., a co-owner, told *Today's Garden Center* magazine. "It looked great, but the problem is, that's telling our customer, 'Hey, I've got nothing different than Home Depot.'"

Unable—and unwilling—to compete on price, Herbert made an overpromise. He decided to make his nursery so visually entrancing, so filled with unique objects for sale, so far ahead of other garden centers in terms of the quality and the total experience, that customers would happily accept premium pricing. "Rather than sell 100 $1 items," Herbert explained, "I'd rather sell 10 $100 items."

And that's just what he did. The pansies go in the back, while up front and all around, in addition to gloriously colorful displays of exotic plants and flowers, are home accessories—one-of-a-kind hanging baskets and pottery, gift items like soaps and lotions, and a wide variety of furniture, indoor and out. Many of the objects are collected in fifteen or so "vignettes," elegant arrangements that customers can sweep up and install at their homes intact for $50,000 or so. Wherever you look is beauty and style: fountains and waterfalls, trees shading a hillside, charming grottoes—all of them for sale.

A few years ago, Roger's managers interviewed customers to find out how they had heard about the place. Three out of five cited a friend or neighbor. With that, Herbert canceled his ads in local papers—the largest share of his marketing budget—and put the money into his payroll, increasing his merchandising team from three to seven. These merchandisers found the items and put them together to create the vignettes. The better the nursery looked, the louder the buzz about it—and the more powerful the word-of-mouth effect.

Traditionally, spring is when nurseries make the most money, but Roger's Gardens has found a way to spread the cheer year-round. The staff goes to great lengths to create incredible holiday displays and products at Halloween and Christmas, which attract visitors and customers from around the country—250,000 during the fourth quarter of the year. Roger's decorates 20 Christmas trees, for example, each of which has an individual theme and up to 2,000 color-coordinated ornaments. Half of its income is now derived from that three-month period.

"As you go up in the value of the product," Herbert noted, "the uniqueness goes up, and the higher your gross margin."

Let's consider some of the lessons to be drawn from the experience of Roger's Gardens:

1. Playing it safe can be risky. When Gavin Herbert Jr. saw that the big-box stores were stealing his nursery's customers, he realized that he had to do something about it. The alternative was to retrench and pray. It was actually safer to make a new overpromise, to stand out with a Product TouchPoint that would make Roger's Gardens a unique, totally differentiated business. It required major changes in every aspect of his operation, and a substantial financial investment, but it paid off handsomely.

2. Cater to the customers you want. To attract people who desire the best and are prepared to pay for it, Herbert recognized that he would have to provide much more than just flowers. He created an elegant environment, a place where they would feel at home. He organized educational activities and fund-raisers that addressed customers' feelings of self-worth. And he sold products that would appeal to their upscale taste. In other words, he understood the variety of factors beyond the product itself that contributed to his Product TouchPoint.

3. Pricing cuts both ways. Unlike his competitors, Herbert was unwilling to continue trying to compete with big-box retailers on price, a losing proposition if ever there was one. He realized that the customers he wanted would not be attracted by bargains. They wanted high value, and they wanted assurance that what they bought at Roger's Gardens was not going to show up on all their friends' patios. To meet those desires, Herbert sent his merchandisers looking for special goods all around the globe, but he also made sure to set a high price on those goods when they made their debut in a vignette. In any consideration of pricing, you need to allow for all kinds of issues. An automatic percentage markup is the wrong way to go.

What's Next?

Product TouchPoints are essential to your success—your product or service is the proximate cause, after all, of any contact between your company and its customers. Other significant TouchPoints demand your attention, too. The chapter that follows discusses how you can tune your System TouchPoints—your Internet and telephonic points of contact, for example—to overdeliver on your overpromise. The goal: to make them so user-friendly that most of your competitors will find them easy to operate.

CHAPTER 6

How Do You Optimize Your System Touchpoints?

A s discussed earlier, I define System TouchPoints as nonhuman interfaces—in other words, contacts between a company and its customers that don't involve direct interaction with the product or service it sells or its people. Think the automated phone system through which subscribers can temporarily stop and restart newspaper delivery without ever speaking to a person; the E-ZPass (East Coast), I-Pass (Illinois), AutoPASS (Norway), and other toll collection systems used on numerous highways and bridges around the world; an ATM, kiosk, or vending machine, or one-click ordering on Amazon.com. If customers come to your retail store or office to do business, these, too, are System TouchPoints.

One of my favorite System TouchPoints makes it possible for you to order food and drinks at a sports event and have them delivered directly to your seat—while you watch an instant re-play of an umpire's questionable call or look up the stats of the other team's punter. Hot dogs, peanuts, and popcorn are part of the fun of going to a game—unless, of course, you're standing in a concession line when the pinch hitter whacks the ball out of the park or the rookie quarterback connects on a Hail Mary pass. But if you're lucky enough to be in one of the growing number of venues that allow you to use your cell phone, PDA, laptop, or other Web-enabled device, you can have food and beverages delivered where you sit without missing any of the action. Among those locations are stadiums used by the Seattle Mariners, San Francisco Giants, and Detroit Tigers.

Nintendo, which owns a majority share of the Mariners, has taken that team's System TouchPoints a step further. Tech-savvy fans at Safeco Field can access updated player stats supplied by MLB.com, a live TV broadcast of the game itself (a boon for those seated high up in the bleachers), multiplayer trivia games, and even a chance to help pick the music played during the game. Sure, you have to rent a DS Lite game console (for $5), download the software, and set up an account using a credit card, but the service itself is simple to use.

In another part of the sports world, National Football League fans in Houston, Miami, Seattle, and Washington, D.C., can use their cell phones to watch pro football games in other cities while sitting in their home-field seats. Telecom giants Sprint and T-Mobile, among others, provide game highlights, fantasy-league action, and other content from the NFL, the National Basketball Association, and media companies. This System Touch-Point between fans and their favorite teams begins the moment a team's technology interacts with that of the customer.

Like all the other TouchPoints, System TouchPoints are moments of truth for a business, an opportunity to fulfill its distinctive overpromise. Doing so successfully requires System TouchPoints to deliver simple, convenient, and trouble-free transactions. Additionally, they must meet two important criteria: consistency and scalability. That is, they must be reliable and capable of accommodating additional demand as your market expands.

System TouchPoints may also offer customers the option of self-service. Whether it's pumping gas, withdrawing cash, shopping online, or paying for groceries, self-service technology allows customers to conduct business when they choose and with little or no wait. At the high end, self-service checkout technology can provide incredible convenience. The New England Stop & Shop supermarket chain offers an array of devices that let shoppers weigh their own produce, order and price deli selections, and check themselves out without the help of store personnel.

The heart of the system is Scan It, a pistol-grip personal scanner with a small screen that lets customers keep track of their selections and gives a running total of the bill. This System TouchPoint is linked to a wireless network by infrared beacons in a store's ceiling.

Here's how it works: You pick up a Scan It from a rack at the front of the store and activate it by swiping your Stop & Shop store discount card. As you walk the aisles choosing assorted items, you simply aim the Scan It at the bar codes and press a button. Besides recording selections and prices, the system tracks the cart's location in the store and alerts you to special bargains keyed to your personal shopping history. When you've gathered all of your groceries, you proceed to one of two automated checkout lines, depending on the number of items being purchased. Scan the bar code atop the checkout device and swipe your store card at the checkout scanner. It reads your list of purchases and tells you how much to pay. Feed a few bills into the slot or swipe your credit card, bag your purchases, and you're on your way.

TouchPoints or TorturePoints?

Despite the clear potential of System TouchPoints as a tool for overdelivering on your overpromise, a caveat is in order: Such efforts can, and often do, go wrong. And when they backfire, they can turn a positive customer experience into a negative one, turning proponents of your brand into critics. In other words, System TouchPoints can become TorturePoints for customers. One sure sign of a TorturePoint: a system designed for the company's benefit, such as cost control, access control, inventory control, or fraud prevention, rather than the customer's benefit, meaning ease of use.

Consider credit card systems as an example. Some actually complicate rather than simplify the process of paying for something. Who hasn't grown impatient standing in a checkout line as a register struggles to recognize another customer's card and spit out a receipt, which a sometimes fumbling customer then has to sign. And when you hand your card to the cashier, you are further delayed. The store's network is down. You've got purchases in hand and are eager to get home. What to do? You have three options: Cool your heels while the clerk fiddles with your card, summon a manager, or abandon your purchases and leave in a huff. None of those solutions is satisfactory.

Similarly, most of us have been infuriated by voice-mail systems designed to ensure that we never speak to a person. Robots with maddeningly chipper voices can usually understand clearly enunciated words and handle routine transactions efficiently. But if a question is complex or doesn't fit into one of the robot's boxes, you're in trouble. If you persist, you may eventually hear a human voice—or, just as likely, you will be cut off. Those in the know can punch in escape codes to bypass voice-mail systems and reach a person. (When the *Wall Street Journal* published two dozen such codes, most of them were immediately changed.) At Visa, for instance, you could call the customer service number, 800-847-2911, press zero two times, hang on despite hearing a message that the response is invalid, and finally get connected. The real question is: Why are customers put through such an ordeal in the first place? Any savings in wages for call center operators is surely more than offset by the cost of customer dissatisfaction and defection. These systems have saved millions of dollars for companies and can be a hassle-saver for customers who just need a flight time or to check a credit card balance, but they should always feature a simple way to get to an operator or customer service representative.

System TouchPoints gone wrong are sometimes no more than Band-Aids applied over time—that is, outdated, half-hearted attempts to correct technical glitches that result in a gumming up of the system. Or they are poorly designed—Web sites that don't provide phone and fax numbers, e-mail and physical addresses, or other obvious contact information; a way to revert to the previous screen; the option to buy more than one of an item; a search engine; a way to compare similar products from obvious competitors; a link to purchase an item online once it's been located; a way to prevent having to enter the same information multiple times; and so on.

Besides such counterproductive System TouchPoints, a marketing approach that's gained currency bears mention. It's the idea that every differentiating brand feature must include a compelling experience, a memorable event that will make customers want to pay a premium for the product or service. In other words, music must play and angels must sing at every single product or service transaction in a person's life.

I don't dispute that Product and Human TouchPoints might sometimes benefit from a showstopper approach, but I'm certain that not every TouchPoint in your arsenal, and particularly not the System TouchPoints, needs to play a starring role. In fact, with System TouchPoints, you almost want them to disappear. Lighting is a critical System TouchPoint in a retail store, but you don't want your customers looking at fixtures. You want them looking at merchandise. Compare it to the experience of reading a book. What matters is the story. You want to be unaware of the "technology" of a printed book. So resist the urge to make each and every System TouchPoint a "Wow!" Use your good judgment to determine which ones work best when they're little noticed or even completely invisible.

Here are examples of companies that are optimizing their System TouchPoints and, in doing so, are supporting and enhancing their overpromises. Each case contains valuable lessons in using System TouchPoints to the best advantage.

Sumerset Houseboats—
Selling a Lifestyle

With an estimated population of slightly more than twelve thousand, you might think the landlocked town of Somerset, Kentucky, is a less than ideal place to sell houseboats costing anywhere from $500,000 to $1 million. That is, until you learn that the Ohio River flows just to the north, the Mississippi runs to the west, and the lakes and reservoirs of the Tennessee Valley Authority are situated to the south and east. Turns out that it's a great location for Sumerset Houseboats.

The company's success is due in part to former CEO Thomas Neckel Sr.'s decision to create a new System TouchPoint, a Web site that turned Sumerset's customers into an extended family. (Neckel, who purchased Sumerset in 1997, has since sold the forty-year-old company to an investment team.) The site's central feature is a series of digital photos of houseboats under construction. Changed daily, the photos allow buyers to keep up with each step of their boat's construction, no matter where they live. By closely linking customers to the company, Sumserset.com reflects and extends Sumerset's unique overpromise, which isn't about boats so much as lifestyle. Or, as Cecil Helton Jr., the site's creator, once put it: The boats are just "a hideaway that lets customers . . . capture time with their friends and family."

Initially, Neckel conceived the site as a display for prospective customers to view design options and receive customized information. But then he had an epiphany: Most anyone building a new house likes to keep tabs on the progress. Wouldn't the same apply to a floating home? That's how Neckel came up with the idea that has done so much to improve customer satisfaction.

At first he thought he would protect his customers' privacy by requiring a password to enter the site. But buyers wanted to see each other's boats to get new design ideas. In a clever compromise, Neckel satisfied everyone by making the photos publicly accessible while identifying them with numbers instead of owners' names. Sumerset.com gets more than forty thousand hits a day, compared to two hundred hits a week for the static Web catalog it replaced.

Besides its obvious popularity with Sumerset's customers, this System TouchPoint had another positive impact as well. Sumerset's employees became more productive. Knowing their works-in-progress were being observed by customers made them want to be seen as moving steadily along. Another invaluable side effect: the almost immediate discovery of errors. For example, when Sumerset's workers began installing the wrong entertainment center in a boat under construction, the customer caught the mistake before it turned into a costly repair problem. "Two weeks later, it would have been major dollars to fix," Helton told *Inc.* magazine. Then, too, allowing buyers to monitor their boats' progress online saves time and money that the company once spent on entertaining customers, who typically made six or seven visits to the plant during the construction process. Follow-up visits have been reduced to a minimum.

Debra and Bruce Wollaber are among the customers delighted with the photo-shoot TouchPoint. After the Wollabers ordered a three-bedroom, two-bath houseboat a few years ago, they logged on daily to follow its construction. On the first day, the gleaming aluminum hull of boat number 22,891 was completed, after which the Wollabers saw the deck being laid, machinery being installed, superstructure being framed, and kitchen and entertainment center being put in. After six weeks, the finished eighteen-by-eighty-six-foot craft set off on a one-day test cruise on the company pond. Initially apprehensive about designing a houseboat, Debra found the process "totally enjoyable," due in no small part to the excitement of watching her boat being built from the hull up.

All in all, this System TouchPoint has yielded handsome returns for Sumerset: Quality and productivity went up, costs went down, and customers sailed away happy. The latter achievement was formally recognized in 2008 when the National Marine Manufacturers Association gave Sumerset its CSI (Customer Satisfaction Index) Award for excellent customer satisfaction in the Sterndrive Houseboats category.

Sumerset is the first houseboat manufacturer to qualify and win the award since the association initiated it in 2001.

Besides showcasing the custom houseboats it builds and the glowing testimonials it receives from satisfied customers, Sumerset's site also operates as a clearinghouse for people buying and selling used houseboats. (On the day I visited Sumerset. com, the used-houseboat offerings ranged from a small, $49,000 boat built by another manufacturer to a larger, $399,000 Sumerset creation.) In fact, what Sumerset has done is to use its unique System TouchPoint to create a houseboating community. As such, Sumerset's bulletin board encourages houseboat owners to share their experiences, publicizes events of interest, and announces the Rendezvous gatherings the company sponsors every year.

These gatherings draw both owners and prospective customers like the Wollabers, who placed their boat order at a Sumerset Rendezvous. For people who are interested but can't attend, Sumerset posts updates of the activities and digital snapshots. The Rendezvous, which would be far less successful without Sumerset.com's support, represents event marketing par excellence and inspires lots of buzz. The site is such an efficient sales tool that Sumerset no longer needs the brokers who used to sell about a third of the boats the company makes each year. That means money previously spent on commissions now goes directly to the bottom line.

Sumerset's imaginative use of its Web site is a powerful illustration of the advantages System TouchPoints have over unpredictable Human TouchPoints. Even the success or failure of Product TouchPoints can hinge on factors over which a business has no control, such as market conditions or consumer trends. As a rule, System TouchPoints are less capricious. Sumerset.com, in particular, exemplifies the TouchPoint ideal because it reliably gives the boat builder's customers experiences and services they can count on. A well-designed and well-tested System TouchPoint puts you in control of interactions with customers and meets the two essential requirements of consistency and scalability.

Sumerset's story and its flourishing Web site offer lessons about optimizing System TouchPoints. Here are three of them:

1. Be flexible and embrace the unexpected. Neckel and Helton devised a simple way to display boats being built without infringing on customer privacy. The unanticipated outcome was that customers began adopting design ideas from other people's boats to their own. Also, when Sumerset's System TouchPoint let the customers view its manufacturing process up close, the company happily used them as unpaid quality control managers.

2. Humanize System TouchPoints to avoid alienating people who prefer to deal with people. Sumerset customers used to visit the factory to check on the progress of their boats. Now, with Sumerset.com's daily pictorial updates, customers are even more involved in the details of construction, but no travel is involved. What's more, the money Sumerset saves on entertaining visiting customers hasn't caused customer relations to decline; quite the opposite.

Making it easy for customers to access and control a System TouchPoint can expand the TouchPoint's value, as it did in the case of the Sumerset customer who asked for specific pictures to be posted and immediately had her wishes granted.

3. Look for ways to expand and leverage System TouchPoints. Sumerset's addition of a used-boat clearinghouse was a natural extension of its houseboat lifestyle overpromise. It draws buyers who might wish to get their feet wet, so to speak, with a less expensive, used houseboat. It also adds a new and helpful service for existing customers who want to trade up. The houseboat gatherings are another powerful tool that strengthens customers' ties to the company and to each other. At the same time, they attract new customers, widening the potential market for used boats and allowing Sumerset to bypass commissioned brokers.

Progressive Goes the Extra Mile

If "other businesses go the extra mile," asked Progressive's Peter Lewis in a *Fast Company* article, "why not an auto-insurance company?" The then chief executive was sincere, but his question was tinged with irony. The insurance business, as Lewis knew full well, is notorious for ever-rising premiums and tortoiselike service. His question was the prelude to a total overhaul at Progressive, the Ohio-based insurance holding company whose major line of business is auto insurance. Lewis wanted to do something about the weeks-, if not months-, long waits that customers endured to get claims resolved.

In 1989, Lewis set out to change the situation by issuing the memo that inaugurated "Immediate Response claims service," a System TouchPoint designed to resolve claims in hours or days. Pushing his idea through despite protests from colleagues, Lewis transformed Progressive from an also-ran into a leader in its industry. In fact, with more than ten million customers, Progressive is the third largest auto insurer in the country, based on premiums written.

Immediate Response means that Progressive springs into action 24/7 to give its customers caring, personal service and support immediately after it's notified of an accident or other loss. The process also empowers claims adjusters to settle a claim on the spot, without having to wait for manager approval.

Converting claims processing into a twenty-four-hour operation inspired Progressive's leaders to rethink nearly every aspect
of the organization. Today, claims offices around the country
forward inquiries and assignments to adjusters. They, in turn,
drive wherever the customer needs them—even to the scene of
an accident—in specially marked SUVs equipped with laptops,
printers, digital cameras, and cell phones. Few people actually
call the company from an accident scene. Still, Progressive man-
dates that all vehicles be inspected within nine hours of an accident report.

The company's Immediate Response program is an outstanding System TouchPoint for customers because it supports the
company's differentiating brand overpromise: to make insurance easy and understandable, with service as fast as customers
need it. Making them feel cared for has helped Progressive leap-
frog competitors, growing premiums from $2 billion in 1994 to
close to $14 billion in 2007. For the year, the company reported
net income of just over a billion dollars, or $1.65 a share diluted,
on total revenues of nearly $15 billion.

Progressive's initial market niche, high-risk auto insurance,
now makes up only about 25 percent of its business. Standard-
risk and preferred coverage policies account for the rest. Progressive insures a wide assortment of personal vehicles, ranging
from motorcycles to the two-wheeled Segway. It also writes
commercial auto and truck policies for small businesses. All are

sold through call centers, on Progressive.com, and by more than thirty thousand independent insurance agencies.

Early on, the company was dismayed to discover that some customers waited days to report accidents. Delays in the adjustment process increase the likelihood that a vehicle will be repaired before a claims adjuster can examine it, and may also help those who choose to invent injuries—not to mention the body shops that pad their bills. To reemphasize the company's commitment to making auto insurance easy and understandable, Progressive developed a claims card. It resembles a credit card, carries the company's toll-free claims number, and has a space for the policy number. It also easily breaks in half so that one piece can be given to the other party involved in an accident. The introduction of the claims card has reduced the time in which customers report incidents from days to hours.

One of Progressive's newest System TouchPoints (a patented first in the industry) introduces true end-to-end service. Called concierge level, it is convenient for customers whose vehicles are still mobile after an accident: They can drive directly to one of fifty-four claims centers in forty-one metropolitan areas, leave their damaged cars, pick up a rental, and know that their cars will be repaired by a Progressive-approved body shop and the work inspected and guaranteed by the company.

Progressive.com is perhaps the company's main System TouchPoint. Within a decade of the Web site's launch in 1995,

Progressive could boast more than ninety-two million unique visitors a year. Potential customers are attracted to the site because they can quickly and easily compare Progressive's premiums to those charged by other insurers. (Incidentally, Progressive holds another patent for its online policy-servicing operations.) After typing in data about his car, a potential customer can get a firm quote on a policy, and by entering his zip code he can get a list of nearby agents who will write the policy. Progressive.com offers easily understood language and strives to "remove the mystery from auto insurance," Toby Alfred, the general manager of Progressive's customer acquisition group, told *PR Newswire*.

Independent agents—who write about 70 percent of Progressive's policies—have their own dedicated site, www.ForAgentsOnly.com. This System TouchPoint enables agents to access information, make changes to current policies, quote new business, submit applications to the company, and accept payments online.

Progressive also has a System TouchPoint that lets registered customers go online and service their own accounts. Accessed via a tab on Progressive.com, policyholders can make payments online and even change policy details. For instance, a policyholder can change an address, add a new driver when a son or daughter gets a license, raise a deductible amount, or lower liability limits to reduce the premium. Customers often go to Progressive.com for "what ifs," the company says: What will happen to my premium if I trade in my Honda Civic for a Toyota Prius? What will be the decrease in my collision premium if I raise the deductible to $500 or $1,000? Some agents bemoan this kind of self-service because it reduces the agent's contact with clients and cuts his or her chances of providing additional service. But the company makes a daily ritual of giving agents a heads-up as soon as one of their customers makes a change, thus giving them a chance to immediately follow up with the customer.

The company's competitors have tried to copy its online innovations, but none has yet been able to match its expertise. One piece of evidence: a 2008 study released by the Customer Respect Group (CRG) in March and Keynote Systems' award to the company in April. CRG put Progressive.com at the top of its list of twenty-two insurance sites based on simplicity of use, support for users' individual needs, quality and speed of response to e-mails, protection of users' personal data, and transparency of processes. And Keynote, which measures users' online experiences on a quarterly basis, crowned Progressive number one in the insurance-carrier segment for the first three months of 2008. It was the company's twelfth such honor since 2000.

The Keynote scorecard gauges a company's e-commerce offerings against industry-specific benchmarks derived from 250 or more best-practice criteria. It cited Progressive.com's excellence in functionality, privacy and security, and quality and availability of features in again placing it at the top of a list of thirteen competitors. Keynote applauded Progressive's revamping of this System TouchPoint, citing its "simplified navigation screen and immediate entry into the quoting application from almost all pages," along with its paperless sales, service options, and the ease with which an independent agent can be located.

And Progressive isn't done yet. At this writing in 2008, the company was awaiting regulatory approval for a national rollout of its MyRate system of usage-based pricing of auto insurance premiums. Using a wireless device that plugs into a car's on-board diagnostic system, customers basically determine their own rate based on how many miles they drive and how and when they drive them. Finally, safe drivers, infrequent drivers, and households with more cars than drivers will also get a break. *Fast Company* magazine dubbed MyRate a 2008 "Fast 50 Reader Favorite."

Progressive's set of System TouchPoints provides at least four lessons:

1. Beat competitors that consistently fail to satisfy customers' basic expectations by designing System TouchPoints that enhance and support a unique over-promise. You will quickly dominate the market, at least until rivals can match your moves, by which time you should have raised the bar even higher. Progressive's decision to cut the usual wait and make claims service

quickly available in person 24/7 was the key to its becoming a leader in auto insurance.

2. Be prepared to change all associated processes substantially when you launch an unusually innovative System TouchPoint. Progressive had to revolutionize its internal processes to support its beefed-up level of service. For example, it had to change the way its adjusters work, adding a fleet of specially equipped vehicles to facilitate on-the-spot resolutions.

A major new System TouchPoint can open the way for more. After Progressive began its Immediate Response system, it discovered troubling delays in claims reporting. To combat this problem it came up with a claims card that carries information facilitating prompt reporting of accidents. The concierge level of service, another new TouchPoint that grew out of the Immediate Response system, lets customers whose vehicles are still operable drive directly to a claims center after an accident. They pick up rental cars and leave the details of the repairs to Progressive.

3. Handle disruptive changes with care. When new System TouchPoints threaten to upset existing procedures, let them—but be sensitive to those most affected by the changes. Agents who feared that Progressive's self-service feature would curtail their relationships with clients were nervous, and rightly so. But by making sure that agents were notified promptly of all such changes, Progressive kept the agents engaged and able to use the occasion to strengthen their contacts with customers.

What's Next

Sumerset and Progressive—these case studies underscore my point that System TouchPoints are among the best ways to support and reinforce a company's differentiating brand promise. They enhance both Product and Human TouchPoints, but without the inherent unpredictability injected by people. Wherever you can effectively substitute System TouchPoints for in-person service, you will bring predictability, reliability, and certainty to the process, and you may be able to cut costs substantially in the process.

But that doesn't mean totally eliminating Human Touch-Points. In some businesses, human contact is critical, and in nearly every line of business, Human TouchPoints, when used in the right places, can be remarkably effective. The next chapter explains why.

CHAPTER 7

How Do You Optimize Your Human Touchpoints?

T hree bald performers, their heads and hands covered in blue greasepaint, cavort onstage. They splash paint, drum on homemade instruments, cut Twinkies with a jigsaw, and catch audience-tossed marshmallows and gumballs in their mouths. But, like Charlie Chaplin or Buster Keaton in the days before movies had sound, the Blue Men are silent entertainers. Using physical stunts and visual gags and interacting with the audience, the performers make fun of abstract art, information overload, and the fallibility of technology. The audience is amused, amazed, and eager to come back for more. They have just witnessed the critically acclaimed Blue Man Group overdelivering on its overpromise to provide unique, thought-provoking, and enormously enjoyable entertainment. What piqued my interest in the group is the skillful way in which the original trio developed its brand by improving and enlarging upon its Human TouchPoints.

Blue Man Group began in 1988, when Chris Wink, Matt Goldman, and Phil Stanton, who were all in their mid-twenties, staged a "funeral for the '80s" in Manhattan's Central Park. They donned bald caps, painted themselves blue, and burned a collection of 1980s memorabilia that they despised, including yuppie characters and Rambo dolls. So well received was that first production that the group put together a stage show that they performed to packed houses at the off-Broadway Astor Place Theatre. The three friends romped through the same routine for twelve hundred performances. Then Stanton cut his hand, and they were forced to bring in an understudy who had never performed the show. To the partners' surprise, he did just fine. New possibilities opened up. The painted anonymity of the Blue Men meant that substitute actors could be hired, and the show could be performed in multiple venues. In other words, because their Human TouchPoint wasn't limited to just a few people, the Blue Man Group was inherently scalable.

In 1995, the group opened a second production in Boston, but it immediately experienced problems. When Goldman, Stanton, and Wink weren't onstage, the production lost its focus. With no written script or formal musical score, the players had been free to improvise, interpreting the performance as they saw fit—but that changed after Boston: The three partners wrote out a detailed set of ideas and moves that all Blue Men have followed since. What had been their own intuitive, nonverbal understanding was codified into an operating manual for the brand's Human TouchPoints.

Reproducing the TouchPoints required more than just a manual, however. The cast had to conform to certain standards, so a hiring policy was developed. As long as they are of similar height and build and have acrobatic ability, the actors can be of any nationality or ethnic group, male or female; so far, one woman has transformed herself into a Blue Man.

A group of performers is not a steel mill or a supermarket chain, but the principles of overpromising and overdelivering are still the same: Businesses succeed by leveraging their Human TouchPoint, which occurs the moment a member of sales, service, or technical staff interacts in person or over the phone with a customer. The degree to which that interaction fulfills a brand overpromise depends on how the customer feels about dealing with an employee. And therein lies a problem: The unpredictability of human emotions has entered the equation, making the Human TouchPoint less reliable than Product and System TouchPoints. The product will likely live up to its design, manufacturing, and delivery standards, which are largely within your control. You can also be relatively confident that the technology you use for dealing with customers will operate consistently and is scalable. Control and consistency can never be guaranteed, however, when it comes to the Human Touch-Point. Even if your employees deliver flawless service, you can't predict a customer's reaction.

Recently one of my clients had a customer complain about a problem. The frontline person apologized profusely on behalf of the business and took full personal responsibility, even though he had nothing to do with the particular transaction. He was willing to replace the product, provide a different product, provide a full refund, or anything else the customer wanted. He concluded by asking, "What would you like me to do?" The customer was outraged that he was given a choice, exclaiming, "Why are you leaving it up to me? You are the customer service person!"

Despite its unpredictability, the Human TouchPoint remains essential to the ongoing mission of overdelivering on a brand overpromise, and people employed in the right ways can bring enormous value to a brand. Numerous occasions arise in which a customer needs a personal touch. When a situation is complicated or ambiguous, when patience, flexibility, and initiative are required to hold on to a customer or win a new one, rely on frontline people to save the day. That's when the Human Touch-Point is the best solution, essential, really, for overdelivering on a brand overpromise.

Beware Overreliance on Human TouchPoints

It's true that Human TouchPoints are critical in virtually every business, but they do have their limits. Many organizations rely on their frontline people more than they should, which implies that other TouchPoints, particularly the System TouchPoint, aren't being optimized.

Look around your business. How much of what your people do must be done by individuals? In many companies, people regularly handle functions that could be consistently delivered more simply, effectively, and less expensively in other ways. Doing so would free up employees to deliver far higher value to customers. Worse yet, they are consigning their company's fate to the vagaries of unpredictable relationships.

The folly of trusting a company's fate to "heroes" is nowhere better exemplified than in the tale of Nordstrom. The Seattle-based upscale clothing chain was a legendary service provider almost since the day in 1901 when John W. Nordstrom first started selling shoes. Nordies, as employees call themselves, thought nothing of custom-suiting a frantic business traveler after lunch in time for dinner, or personally delivering shoes to a customer a hundred miles away because overnight mail service would be too slow.

This is what I call heroics-based customer service, and it was appropriate and appreciated when Nordstrom served a small, elite clientele willing to pay for the heroics. But for big companies in mass markets with thousands of employees it requires exacting recruiting, training, and support systems. Just think about it: How strong is a business model predicated on delivering heroic service? And where do you find all those people willing to do the heroics on their personal time? Regression to the mean ensures that even starting out with all heroes, scaling will result in more and more nonheroes being hired, weakening the fulfillment of the overpromise.

Nordstrom itself is a case in point. As it expanded rapidly in recent years—it now has 160 stores in 28 states, 106 of which are full-line stores—it tried in vain to maintain its heroic customer service, ignoring the fact that it was increasingly unable to keep its overpromise of exceptional personal service. As a result, overall customer service declined. Labor shortages made good (read: heroic) salespeople hard to find. Staffers sued the chain for unpaid overtime and alleged harassment as managers pushed to meet hourly sales quotas; Nordstrom settled the suit for $22 million. Meantime, the chain's once bouncy image turned stodgy. Intent on boosting its share price to finance expansion, Nordstrom had neglected its emotional ties to younger customers, who jumped ship. Earnings plunged 50 percent in fiscal 2001.

Nordstrom continues to add still more stores, but realizes

that revitalized, consistent customer service aimed at both older and younger generations is critical, if not the ticket for its survival. What is clearly required is a full-scale rebirth of consistently good service and selection for all of the company's customers. As I am writing this, Nordstrom's rejuvenated overpromise, supported by a more realistic Human TouchPoint, is working: In the fiscal year that ended February 2, 2008, the retailer's net income increased to $715 million, up 5.5 percent from $628 million earned the year before, and up a healthy 30 percent from the over $551 million posted in fiscal 2006. The all-important same-store sales grew for the sixth year in a row, increasing nearly 4 percent on top of a 7.5 percent increase in 2006 and a 6 percent increase in 2005.

Recognizing the pros and cons of Human TouchPoints, you must assess where you stand. Have you assigned sufficient resources to support your salespeople and service representatives? Does your company's culture inspire them to achieve? Are you providing the right kind of environment and incentives? Have you developed the best hiring and training programs in your market?

The pages ahead contain case histories of companies that, like the Blue Man Group, have designed superb Human Touch-Points to help fulfill their brand overpromises, and each has lessons to teach. In fact, let's begin with those men in blue to see what your business can take away from their experiences:

1. Prepare the script. If you want your frontline people to behave in a particular manner—and surely you do—heed Blue Man's example and give them a script to follow. Make it as detailed as you think necessary, but I would err on the side of giving too much rather than too little information. It should spell out what each customer interaction should look like, sound like, and feel like. Sure, you want to leave room for intelligent and intuitive experimentation by your sales and service people, but you also want them to know when and why they are deviating from the norm. You must make the implicit explicit. When Chris Wink and his partners worked out their operating manual, it was 132 pages long. It was full of insights ("the Blue Men are not aliens") and literary and theatrical references. Your version is likely to be more prosaic, and shorter, but the goal is the same: to provide consistency and scalability at the Human TouchPoint.

2. Hire to the script. Any normally capable person can read the manual and follow directions. For your Human TouchPoint to reach its full potential, you need to hire and train people who will live your overpromise-aligned manual. Blue Man Group looks for people who understand and embody the essential character of their roles, people who can connect with their audiences. You should do the same. Don't hire someone who can simply "act" friendly and helpful. The characteristics you seek should be second nature to the people you hire—no acting involved. In other words, if you want your sales representatives to maintain a smiling, upbeat presence, you better be certain that those you hire have naturally pleasant, optimistic personalities. Qualities like that cannot be faked over the long haul. In fact, skillful hiring is the best and easiest way to improve every aspect of your company—from its culture to its everyday performance to its brand overpromise.

3. Train to the script. Newcomers to the ranks of your frontline staff must be trained to master your manual for overdelivering just as Blue Man newcomers are trained in the actions and ideas that define a Blue Man performance. Your new salespeople should also be indoctrinated in the spirit that informs the script and the brand overpromise—in other words, they must understand the context, not just the text.

So far, we've concentrated on newcomers, but don't forget about veterans. All too often, companies ignore the very real need to retrain experienced frontline staffers. Winning companies don't take anything or anyone for granted. They invest in retraining to keep everyone up to date and in sync with rejuve-nated brand promises. It should come as no surprise that the longer an employee stays in a job, the more bad habits and atti-tudes he or she is likely to pick up.

The best companies I have studied invest heavily in training. The Container Store is one of these best-of-breed businesses. Its veteran full-time employees receive 160 hours of training each year. Regular retraining can help keep your Human TouchPoint from drifting out of line with your overpromise.

The Richard Petty Driving Experience

Strapped into the race car's driver seat, 600 horses raring to go, you sit watching the flagman up ahead. He finally gives you the "go" sign and you ease up on the clutch while feeding her gas. The car glides along an oval track where some of the greatest names in NASCAR history have made their marks. Gradually, you move up through the gears until you reach fourth, then you floor it. The engine roar is deafening. The forward thrust almost crushes you in your seat. As your speed climbs, the centrifugal force pushes you hard to the right: 100 . . . 125 . . . 140 . . . 165 mph.

That's the ultimate thrill the Richard Petty Driving Experi-ence offers at twenty-five tracks around the country. Petty is a seven-time NASCAR national champion in a sport whose popularity has exploded over the past decade and a half, and his Concord, North Carolina–based company has flourished right along with it. Petty's 130,000 paying customers, both drivers and passengers, log over three million track miles a year. From the moment you climb into your fire suit to the moment you squeeze out of the car and find out your fastest lap speed, every step has been carefully calculated to give you a realistic sense of what it's like to be a NASCAR driver. The vehicle you drive duplicates the real thing in appearance and performance, except for somewhat lower horsepower. Your name is announced over the track's public address system as you prepare to drive. There is no passing—for safety's sake, every driver must follow an instructor's car around the track. But once you demonstrate the ability to control your car and maintain the proper distance from the lead vehicle, you can drive as fast as the instructor and the particular track permit.

Before you're allowed anywhere near a racing car, though, you're put through a lengthy training process. You watch a video in which the King—Petty's track nickname—warns you of the potential hazards ahead. The cars are fast: They can get away from you quickly and spin easily if you're not careful. An instructor drives you around the track in a van, pointing out the cones that alert you when to take your foot off the gas and when to accelerate. After a few more driving tips, you are introduced to your car. You learn how to shift and how to operate the fire extinguisher system. A track employee helps get you into the driver's seat, helmeted, and strapped in. But after he starts the engine, you are on your own.

The company has grown tremendously over the eighteen years since it first put the public into racing cars. Petty has developed a powerful brand overpromise—to provide safe, reliable, authentic motor-sports entertainment—and overdelivered on it admirably. (Not one of the company's many thousands of customers has sustained an injury.) It has built its brand by first identifying thirty-one TouchPoints at which it interacts with customers, and then devising a quality assurance process around each of them. And by investing virtually all of its resources in improving its customers' experience, the company has avoided major outlays for advertising and promotion. It relies instead on word of mouth.

One of the most important of the company's customer-centric TouchPoints is its call center, which handles more than 150,000 calls annually. Some years ago, new employees at this Human TouchPoint were trained by veterans who sat down with the newcomers and showed them what to do and how to do it. The operators then tried their hand at the process, and supervisors gave them a bit of feedback. The results, however, were very uneven, and the training period sometimes stretched over three or four weeks.

Then Petty began using a computer-based training tool called

Communication Coach, developed by Success Sciences of Tampa, Florida, a company that specializes in the human element of the customer experience. This technology allows new hires to listen to and study dozens of simulated conversations in which callers receive ideal treatment from employees. The conversations are completely customized to the culture and brand promise of the client company, reflecting its views on what should be said, in what order, and how. For example, the tone of the employee's voice and the speed and volume of delivery are dictated by the client company and the product or service it is offering. Trainees record their own practice sessions responding to callers, and then toggle back and forth between the model and their own versions, noting differences along the way. This comparison feature also enables a trainee's supervisor to provide precisely focused feedback and reinforcement. In addition, the Communication Coach teaches new call center employees how to navigate through the company's software system and provides information about the company's products, policies, and procedures.

Frank Vari, Petty's executive vice president, spells out the business benefits of the Communication Coach approach. "In the old days," he said, "you were always like, okay, I think they can do the job. You had your fingers crossed. Now we know for certain that they will do the job, and do it well." And instead of three or four weeks, the computer training takes just two.

Vari also noted a positive change in the operators' attitudes. "Far more than in the past, they're trying to understand what individual customers need and trying to find ways to drive the sale."

Clearly, the company's Human TouchPoint has benefited enormously from its use of a computer training program. Here are three lessons drawn from the Petty company's experience:

1. Consistency counts. The Petty operation started with the romantic and dramatic idea of giving racing fans a chance to experience firsthand some of the thrills of being a NASCAR driver. To make sure that happened for every customer every time, the company had to build the right kind of cars and design a process that would be safe for customers, instructors, and the cars themselves. It also had to convince tracks around the country to welcome the program. Finally, it had to fashion a Human TouchPoint, supported by technology, that would seamlessly lead customers through the other TouchPoints of the experience, start to finish. Once its method was developed, the company made sure it would be followed to the letter at all its sites. "It's no different from McDonald's," Frank Vari says. "We want to make sure you have the same great experience wherever you go. We want repeat customers, and we get them."

2. Recognize the limits of technology. As potent as computer training can be in preparing frontline employees for their assignments, it can't do the whole job. As the Petty Driving Experience discovered, you and your managers will in the end have to judge whether trainees are meeting your standards of performance. Monitor how trainees are doing with selected software, and provide whatever personal training is necessary.

3. Technological tools have their place in supporting Human TouchPoints, but they also have their limits. They can be ingenious, cost-effective, and thorough, but no computer program can give the individual attention and reinforcement a frontline employee may need to get the most out of the training. In other words, don't expect technology to totally eliminate the need for human interaction in training, coaching, and leadership. The role of software is to shorten the learning cycle and bring much-needed consistency to the Human TouchPoint.

4. Customize. As a general rule, building an effective TouchPoint of any kind requires tailoring the process to your company, your overpromise, and the particular customers you're trying to reach. In Frank Vari's view, that was the key to the success at Petty: "We customized the scenarios to handle the situations that we were dealing with, and to handle our unique challenges. That's what made the difference." Customers in every business pose different sorts of questions and problems, and the Human TouchPoints must be form fitted.

The Container Store—
The Best Place to Work

Everyone agrees that engaging interpersonal interactions are a basic ingredient of a breakthrough Human TouchPoint. The Container Store is a role model for that kind of service. The Dallas-based retail chain, which offers more than ten thousand storage and organization products, grounds its brand promise in this simple reality: The company hires fewer frontline people than its competitors, trains and coaches them superbly, and pays them from 50 to 100 percent more than the going industry average.

Kip Tindell, the company's cofounder and chief executive, would seem to agree: "A funny thing happens when you take the time to educate your employees, pay them well, and treat them as equals," he told *Workforce* magazine. "You end up with extremely motivated and enthusiastic people." The kind of people who make customers and suppliers happy, too, and all these good feelings end up fattening the bottom line, thereby bringing great joy and good feelings to shareholders. It's simple, really. But if the bottom line begins to crowd employees out of the picture, the recipe is ruined. Adherence to the magic formula has turned the Container Store into a forty-three-store, privately owned empire that stretches across the country and has achieved sales growth of 15 to 20 percent every year since it opened for business thirty years ago. For 2007, that growth translated into revenues of $600 million.

Walk into a Container Store and you enter a world very different from any other retail environment. Instead of shoes, dresses, or television sets, there are shelves, racks, bags, and boxes arranged in rooms—kitchen, closet, office, laundry. Instead of salespeople who ignore you, the Container Store is staffed by smiling, friendly folks in blue aprons who are happy to greet you and seem to enjoy their jobs. They also listen carefully, respond intelligently, and suggest ingenious space- and time-saving solutions designed to simplify your life.

Tindell and partner Garrett Boone, the chairman emeritus, opened the first Container Store in Dallas in 1978. It wasn't all smooth sailing. They had a computerized inventory system that didn't work and headaches caused by too much growth too fast. The realization that they were also hiring the wrong people led to the development of a set of principles that have guided the company and its employees ever since. Among them:

- Fill the other guy's basket to the brim; making money then becomes an easy proposition.

- Apply the Golden Rule in all encounters, creating an environment of trust with customers, vendors, and fellow employees.

- Create a sense of excitement in every store.

- Be Gumby. The reference is to the corporation's mascot, the green toy notable for its incredible flexibility, but the message is a familiar one: Make the implicit explicit.

- Train intensely so that your intuitive leaps are based upon research, not guesswork.

All first-year, full-time Container Store employees receive 241 hours of training, as compared to the industry average of 8; new part-timers get 150 hours of training. All new employees—including office staff—spend their first week working in a store. As mentioned earlier, veteran full-timers get an average of 160 hours of training each year. Very little turnover is what makes such intensive training affordable for the company. At the Container Store, the turnover rate for all full-time employees is 10 percent and for part-timers, 30 to 35 percent. Contrast that to an industry average of 70 percent.

Intensive, hands-on training is particularly important at the Container Store because of the multitude of products it offers and the "man in the desert," comprehensive-solutions principle it espouses. A man lost in the desert for days may ask rescuers for water, but he also needs food, a chance to call his family, a place to sleep. By the same token, a customer might ask just for something to keep his shirts in, but may actually need to have his whole closet reorganized. So when approaching a customer's problem, employees are encouraged to think big and expand the boundaries in order to devise a great solution that not only wows the customer but, as it usually turns out, also sells more products. The Container Store's frontline people are well prepared to recognize any need and satisfy it.

An emotional response is what Container Store employees are after. What evokes that emotional response is the relationship its sales reps establish at the Human TouchPoint, which is in turn a function of their very positive attitudes toward their jobs and their company. For several years, the Container Store has been at or near the top of *Fortune* magazine's list of "100 Best Companies to Work For." A conversation with the company's employees explains why. They talk about wanting to come to work, about enjoying the interaction with customers, about a culture in which "people care about each other."

Sales representatives are encouraged to make their own decisions when they work with customers, and if the customer's problem is a complex one, frontline people respond as a team, discussing various ideas and arriving at a unique solution. Having hired the best people, paid them handsomely, trained them thoroughly, and indoctrinated them in the culture, the company expects them to perform at their peak—and they do.

Here are some lessons drawn from the Container Store experience to help you make the most of your Human TouchPoints:

1. Put it on paper. Most companies do not live up to their brand promises. A company's leaders need to determine the essence of their brand, all the things that make it distinctive, and then make sure that the overpromise is thoroughly understood and accepted by their frontline employees. The Container Store, which promises unparalleled service in helping customers to find unique storage ideas, achieves this goal in part by having a set of principles that trainers and managers discuss with newcomers. When the Human TouchPoint truly reflects the overpromise, you will realize a new level of sales and profitability.

2. Hire top talent. There's no denying it's expensive, not only because it can mean higher salaries, but also because you must create an environment that will make these kinds of employees want to stay around. But, as the Container Store's experience shows, you can recoup your investment by decreasing turnover and increasing productivity and sales. The work ethic of the frontline people, combined with their commitment to teamwork, enables the Container Store to upgrade the level of its Human TouchPoint while staffing its outlets with far fewer sales representatives than is typical in its industry.

3. Invest in training. What you spend on top talent will be wasted unless you provide the training and education that will perfect your Human TouchPoints. New employees need to know that you want something more than just getting the job done; you want it done magnificently. You must teach your frontline people what your organization's overpromise means and exactly how they should overdeliver on it. Don't leave it to their imaginations. Spell it out.

At the Container Store, new hires are taught how the thousands of products can be manipulated to answer individual customers' needs. The training starts by placing newcomers in the stores so they can see firsthand how sales representatives help customers; it continues in group classes and one-on-one tutorials. Even seasoned veterans receive instruction to bring them up to date on the newest products and sales approaches.

A statistic that I genuinely love is this: In 2006, the Container Store won mention in over fourteen hundred print articles and its employees and products appeared in two hundred television segments. Turns out those well-trained and well-paid Container Store employees are sought-after experts by the media. How's that for a pay-back on training costs?

4. Focus on values. It is crucial to create an environ-ment of mutual trust. The Container Store incorpo-rates that goal in its principles, at the center of which is the Golden Rule: Trust between leaders and employees allows management to redirect a frontline person's energy with-out incurring anger. It also allows an employee to experi-ment with new ideas without fear of punishment if the initiative doesn't pan out. Trust between employees en-ables productive teamwork without competitive rancor, and putting salespeople on a salary (as opposed to a com-mission) removes any reason to feel jealous over another's success. Employees are also kept informed about the state of the business and are consulted before key decisions are made. They see that the generous benefits and salaries, as well as the recognition of special achievement, are distrib-uted fairly.

5. Leave them alone. Once you have hired and trained the very best people you can find and have instilled them with your company's values, they will be better

equipped than you or your managers to help customers. Nothing should hinder them from exercising their knowledge, intuition, and initiative. At the Container Store, the Human TouchPoint works best when sales and service people are encouraged to think like owners, improving existing approaches and devising new ones on the spot. Garrett Boone tells of a salesman in Maryland who discovered, while checking out a customer, that the closets in the woman's new home were completely disorganized. The salesman closed the register and set about planning new closets for her. At a store in Chicago, Boone told a magazine writer, a customer's car seat got ripped when the just-purchased items were being placed in her car. When the saleswoman heard what happened, she immediately took cash from the register and paid the customer for the damage. Top-notch frontline people need the freedom to do their jobs.

In mid-2007, Leonard Green & Partners, a private equity firm that specializes in retail companies, bought majority control of the Container Store. Their promise to preserve the chain's singular culture has been honored thus far. And why not, when that culture lies at the heart of Container Store's amazing success?

Hire the Right People

As the case studies in this chapter suggest, there is no one-size-fits-all personality type that is right for every company. Sure, intelligence and a courteous and respectful demeanor are critical when dealing face-to-face with customers. But what other characteristics should you look for in a frontline hire? For one thing, you are not simply trying to find someone who will fit into your organization; the goal is to identify people who have the capacity to become outstanding, world-class performers in a manner that is aligned with your over-promise.

For instance, Microsoft is looking for outstanding problem solvers, and their screening process is designed to identify just those people. Southwest Airlines wants people who love connecting with and serving other people. Patagonia recruits individuals who are passionate about the planet and environmentally responsible outdoor activities. Starbucks recruits "partners" who love everything about coffee. Imagine what would happen if these companies swapped recruiting strategies. Before you start recruiting, clearly define the characteristics that will enable your team to easily overdeliver on your company's over-promise.

To achieve this goal, adopt a careful, analytical hiring policy.

I suggest developing in-depth, job-specific profiles of the kind of people you want at your Human TouchPoint. The frontline associate should be eager and capable of learning the job and should truly enjoy engaging with and helping other people; the supervisor should be eager to and capable of teaching and mentoring rather than policing. In both cases, start by creating a master profile based on your current top performers. They have already forged a template for success in your specific environment with your customers. Then compare the candidates' results with those of your top performers and include this data, along with personal interviews, references, and other criteria, in your overall assessment of the applicant.

The master profile will include standard information such as education, work experience, and skill levels, and it should also pinpoint personal beliefs and attitudes. What a person thinks about herself is one example; what she's capable of learning to do is another. If technical skills or industry knowledge is required, be sure the applicant has both the interest and the aptitude to pick them up.

One often overlooked but essential part of the hiring process is to have the candidate preview the job slot. Make sure she is clear about the nature of the work and how she would spend her day. The more a new hire knows about the position, the more likely you are to avoid the brisk employee turnover that kills customer satisfaction and corporate profitability. If part of the job is making collection calls to people in difficult financial straits and she hates the idea of doing it, she can turn down the position instead of quitting after she's been hired and trained.

Some companies present job candidates with descriptions of circumstances they will face and ask them to choose how they would handle the situation from among several options. Potential call center operators are asked to listen to actual recorded customer calls and sort out their complaints. The candidates' untutored answers may reveal attitudes you should know about, but the point is to make the potential hires fully aware of what the job entails.

Train Them the Right Way

No matter how thoroughly new hires have been briefed, no matter how carefully they've been tested, it's still a gamble. To hedge your bets, make absolutely certain that new frontline employees are expertly trained to overdeliver at your Human TouchPoint. From what I've seen, most companies fail in this regard.

To guarantee that frontline hires are primed for their positions, define what the customer experience should look like, sound like, and feel like at each critical TouchPoint. Then define what role the front line will play in overdelivering on the overpromise. In other words, what should they be thinking, saying, and doing to create the desired customer experience?

To begin with, newcomers to a company need to understand how their assignment fits into the company's overall functioning. As in any organization, military or civilian, business success depends upon the actions of individual members of the group, and frontline people receive job satisfaction from knowing that everyone's efforts, up and down the supply chain, culminate in the front line's job performance. The sales and service people are handed the product with the expectation that it will be presented appropriately to the customer. Frontline people should be made to appreciate that their performance will ultimately determine the size of everyone's paycheck as well as the company's fate.

New hires also need to be instructed about the why of their jobs—that is, the various contexts within which they will be operating: the competitive, the environmental, the departmental, or the divisional context, to name just a few.

New hires should be encouraged to think like owners, to take the initiative in looking for new and better ways to do their job— always with the understanding that they will not be punished or humiliated if such attempts fail. Familiarity with all of the culture's values is important for new hires, but emphasize that having positive interactions with customers is a special priority. A company dedicated to developing a peerless Human TouchPoint will not impede an employee's desire to help customers by imposing a rigid set of rules.

Now that you know how to find the right people and how to train them once they're hired, you are on your way to optimizing your Human TouchPoint. But I must add: No matter how well you do your job and how good your Human TouchPoint becomes at any given moment, you cannot afford to relax for long. Business is all about change. The only way to stay on top of the situation, to be sure that your frontline people are in tune with your overpromise, and that your overpromise is in tune with your market, is to continuously monitor both frontline people and your customers.

Some years ago, the leaders of Revco Drug Stores (now part of the CVS Caremark) were determined to improve their Human TouchPoint, so they asked themselves: What do we want every customer to experience in every encounter he or she has with our stores? In other words, how can we promote better customer relations?

The senior managers decided upon three very basic things they wanted frontline people to do: Greet every customer entering a Revco store, offer help to any customer searching for an item, and look every customer in the eye when addressing him or her. The slogan for the new program was, appropriately enough, "Every customer, every time." Each store manager received a guide that suggested ways of effectively communicating the changes.

Weeks later, Revco sent anonymous company shoppers to the

stores to measure compliance with the new directive. The company also measured public reaction to the changes, keeping track of commendations and complaints from customers. Within a short time, Revco found that compliance was averaging 90 percent, and the commendation/complaint ratio had tilted drastically toward commendation. The company made sure that the measures of customer reaction were shared with its frontline people to encourage them to persevere with the successful new approach. And, periodically, Revco repeated the same monitoring tactic.

Revco knew—and you should too—that what happens at the Human TouchPoint is too important to leave to chance.

What's Next?

No matter how you slice it, Human TouchPoints are unpredictable. But as the Blue Man Group, the Richard Petty Driving Experience, the Container Store, and the other companies highlighted in this chapter prove, the right people with the proper training are irreplaceable in certain situations. And their unpredictability can even be an asset: Think of the Container Store employee who promptly took cash from the register to repay a customer for damage to her car. The frontline employee's quick—but unpredictable—reaction surely earned the gratitude and loyalty of a customer who might otherwise have waited weeks or months for reimbursement—if it ever came at all.

If your overpromise is one that would benefit from the human touch, my advice is to manage your frontline people carefully and use them wisely—just don't make the mistake of relying too heavily on this single TouchPoint.

Some companies manage to achieve an almost perfect equilibrium among Product, System, and Human TouchPoints. The next chapter takes an up-close look at the secrets of the Japanese carmaker Toyota, whose Lexus division is the unrivaled champion of TouchPoint Branding. Lexus hums along from strength to strength, meshing its Product, System, and Human Touch-Points in a finely calibrated procedure that overpromises and overdelivers with flawless consistency.

CHAPTER 8

A Case in Touchpoint: Lexus

A name can be a single word or syllable or a complex list describing origins, occupations, or even birth order. But whether one word or many, names define us and distinguish us from each other. And as every boy named Sue would surely attest, names can influence not only the way others see us, but also how we see ourselves. In short, names can pack a powerful punch.

So, too, for automobiles.

Names and other defining words are a critical Product Touch-Point that begins to express the emotional bond a car's owners will feel for it. Brands like Buick, Chrysler, and Ford began with the founder's name and acquired emotional resonance over time. Newer nameplates are often a made-up string of syllables that together evoke a feeling—hopefully the one the creators had in mind. Chevrolet infamously named its Nova to signify new and brilliant. Unfortunately, Spanish-speaking drivers interpreted Nova as *no va*, meaning "It doesn't go."

Aware of the pitfalls, Toyota managers spent weeks pondering a list of 219 names dreamed up by Lippincott & Margulies, a New York image consultant, for the new luxury-car model the Japanese manufacturer was going to debut in 1989. The suggestions ranged from Calibre and Chaparel to Vectre and Verone, but the favorite was Alexis. At a marketing meeting in Los Angeles, however, then corporate marketing manager George Borst pointed out that Alexis was the name of the demanding diva played by actress Joan Collins in *Dynasty*, a popular television series at the time. With that, John French, the car's project manager, began to doodle the name on a notepad, minus the A. The spelling soon evolved from Lexis to Lexus, suggesting both the Latin *luxus* (luxury) and the French *luxe* (sumptuous). The result was an invention that perfectly evoked the image the car's creators were seeking—a new, more contemporary expression of luxury.

Then, when "green" became a watchword of the new millennium, Toyota/Lexus presciently and cleverly spent $100 million to make "hybrid" a household term while staking out its own position as the worldwide leader in environmentally conscious motoring. In the United States, it leveraged that double play by joining forces with the Los Angeles–based Environmental Media Association (EMA), a powerful nonprofit group that enlists television, film, and music personalities to help spread environmental awareness. If you've watched an entertainment awards show on television recently and noted a parade of stars arriving in a Lexus hybrid instead of a gas-guzzling limo, the credit goes to EMA.

And in Europe, where Lexus has had a hard time making inroads among the homegrown Audis, BMWs, and Mercedes, the brand, largely thanks to its Product TouchPoint, is starting to close the gap: Lexus's European sales jumped by 76 percent in 2006, and Toyota expects the trend to continue—especially since its European competitors have been slow to embrace hybrids, favoring diesel technology instead. The Lexus brand manager in Europe has called hybrids "our breakthrough."

Long before Toyota named its Lexus brand or even dreamed of hybrids, the car had already traveled a long road. The Lexus journey began early in 1983, when Yuki Togo, head of Toyota's U.S. division, flew to Tokyo to try to persuade the company's directors to enter the luxury-car market. A victory in that hotly contested field, Togo argued, could position Toyota as a leader in the whole U.S. market. And "if [we] could earn the badge of 'No. 1' in this huge market," Togo went on, "it would send reverberations throughout the world."

A fifteen-man planning committee was named, and its marching orders were sweeping. The car, code-named Circle F (for flagship), would be a closely guarded secret whose research and development would take years. It would not be built on the cheap, using an existing Toyota platform; rather, it would be new from the wheels up. No limits were placed on either the time or money devoted to it. That commitment was vital, for when you set out to be the best, you must be ready to do whatever it takes to get there.

Equally important, the project began with the kind of disciplined market research that is essential to effective overpromising and overdelivering. In a simple yet breathtaking approach, Toyota decided that to build a luxury car for the U.S. market it first had to understand what is unique about the concept of luxury in America. The Japanese precept of *genchi genbutsu*—go look, go see—became its guide.

In April 1985, a team of twenty designers and engineers flew off to begin a total immersion in luxurious American living, with orders from Togo to learn everything they could about the life and values of high-end buyers. "You cannot create a 'child of America' unless you understand Americans," he said. "What does a car mean to them? How do they use it? How do they feel when they ride in a car? How does a well-to-do lady get into an automobile with her fur coat on?"

Moving into a large house overlooking the ocean at Laguna

Beach, California, an hour south of Los Angeles, the team began a five-month quest. They visited country clubs, upscale malls, youth soccer leagues, and chic restaurants. They saw men tossing golf bags into Jaguars, women ferrying kids in Benzes and Volvos, and valets parking exotic sports cars. The Toyota team fanned out to observe focus groups of luxury consumers in San Francisco, Denver, Houston, New York, and Miami. In suburban Chicago, they videotaped a wealthy woman as she walked through her home describing her tastes and values, and again as she drove her Jaguar through her community and talked about her neighbors, their houses, and their customs. The tape was played in Japan for hundreds of Toyota designers and engineers. Finally, a consensus was reached: The taste of the American luxury consumer was basically European, but brighter, warmer, and more approachable.

The team returned to Japan, except for five designers who stayed behind in California to begin building clay models of the Lexus. "We couldn't have designed this car in Japan and made it look the way we wanted it to look in America," said Kunihiro Uchida, who oversaw the car's exterior design. "Buildings, the width of streets, other cars on the road, even the vegetation . . . they all affect how a car looks."

Initially, the design team was a bit daunted by the competition. Jaguar, BMW, and Mercedes had recently established solid beachheads in a market long dominated by Lincoln and Cadillac, gaining cachet among more sophisticated buyers who viewed the American offerings as somewhat bulgy and overstuffed, certainly not nimble. The Europeans had exploited the chinks in the American armor, and Toyota wondered how it might compete against the hard-charging invaders.

Auto-industry shoptalk provided at least a partial answer. For years insiders had wisecracked that luxury-car drivers had to "suffer the badge," meaning that, if they wanted the brand's prestige, they had to endure the mechanical shortcomings of the cars and the snobbish attitude of the dealers, who patronized customers and provided slow, offhand service. Early on, Lexus decided it would exploit this weakness. Flawless performance (a Product TouchPoint) and an unprecedented level of personal service (a Human TouchPoint) would be key elements of the Lexus brand promise.

The promise to be "better than the best in the world" was first roughed out by Eiji Toyoda. But one day in 1987, two full years before the first Lexus appeared in a showroom, then general manager Dave Illingworth dictated an inspired refinement of Toyoda's order that became the Lexus Covenant. Now it's carved in granite at the division's headquarters and etched into the frontal lobe of every Lexus manager, salesperson, and mechanic:

Lexus will enter the most competitive, prestigious automobile race in the world. Over 50 years of Toyota automotive experience has culminated in the creation of Lexus cars. They will be the finest cars ever built.

Lexus will win the race because: Lexus will do it right from the start. Lexus will have the finest dealer network in the industry. Lexus will treat each customer as we would a guest in our home.

If you think you can't, you won't. If you think you can, you will. We can, we will.

"[T]he finest cars ever built . . . do it right from the start . . . treat each customer as we would a guest in our home"—the summary statement of which is the Lexus brand promise— overpromise in my lexicon—the passionate pursuit of perfection. And by translating that passionate pursuit into a series of Product, System, and Human TouchPoints, Lexus has achieved ongoing success.

Product TouchPoints, the Lexus Way

Lexus has overdelivered on its overpromise, as the numbers make clear. From first-year sales of 16,000 units in 1989, Lexus sales soared to 322,434 in 2007, when it was the top-selling luxury nameplate in the United States for the eighth year in a row. Its claim to be the finest car in the world is backed up by an endless string of awards from the automotive press. In 2007, for instance, the prestigious J.D. Power & Associates bestowed its coveted Gold Award on Lexus for the seventh straight year, giving it an unbroken string of trophies since it first became eligible for consideration.

From the company's viewpoint, however, the most telling measure is its success in beating the Europeans on American turf: In the brand's first two years, fully 45 percent of its customers traded in a European car for their new Lexus. The figure has dropped since then, mainly because Lexus retains 63 percent of its customers—the second highest loyalty rate of any nameplate; only parent Toyota beats it at 65 percent. No wonder BMW, Jaguar, and Mercedes are on the defensive—and not just in the United States. With Lexus's prescient push into the hybrid field, environmentally conscious Europeans are taking a closer look.

The first reason for the Lexus's success, of course, is the product itself and the string of TouchPoints that define it. Among them is an innovation that came from a member of the initial design team, Michikazu Masu. Masu's daughter, who rode in a carpool to her California school, asked him why she slid forward in her seat every time her classmate's mother hit the brakes of her Mercedes. Masu immediately realized that the interiors of German cars were too stiff. If riding in a Cadillac was like sinking into a divan, riding in a Mercedes was like sitting in a stiff-backed chair. Lexus could exploit this weakness in European design by finding middle ground.

Another epiphany came when Masu held a garage sale and discovered that the upscale buyers were more intrigued by the map to his house than by the merchandise. The visitors praised the map he had drawn as "simple, clean, and smart." Masu would not have used those words to describe the luxury-car market, but now he thought otherwise. Simple, clean, and smart became the Lexus watchwords for key design features, large and small.

For customers, Lexus's first Product TouchPoint is the feeling they get when they slide into the driver's seat—the unspoken "aah" that comes with experiencing the height of luxury. That feeling is reinforced by a wealth of subtle details, ranging from buttery-soft leather seats and the rich gleam of the wood-trimmed interior to the Lexus's hushed, silky ride and smooth handling. All of these details are the product of never-ending questioning, research, testing, and reworking. Nothing is too small to escape notice. When Toyota's interior designers were testing different steering wheels, for example, they bought plastic press-on fingernails to get a sense of how American women might experience various design options. The same level of interest and intensity goes into every square inch of every Lexus, inside and out.

Lexus pursues perfection just as painstakingly when it comes to the actual production of its cars. A sure sign of Lexus's unwavering commitment to quality came in the first months of production in 1988, when cars began arriving in California with noisy fan belts. Another company might well have decided to fix the problem on the fly, continuing production, shipping the cars, and replacing the defective parts at the dealerships. But Lexus is not just another car company. It stopped the line and shipped no cars from Japan until their belts were quiet.

Over time, the car's Product TouchPoints have evolved to reflect both the customers' changing tastes and the company's widening range of product choices. From its original LS 400 model, Lexus has grown to an eight-model line that ranges from quietly luxurious to performance-oriented to environmentally conscious. Models have been developed for the entry- and midlevel luxury buyer as well as for bigger spenders. The 1998 GS, the world's fastest automatic-transmission sedan, was produced as a head-on challenge to BMW, and Lexus gave birth to the luxury crossover market with its first SUV, the RX 300. Named *Motor Trend* magazine's sport utility of the year when it was introduced in 1998, the RX 300 quickly became a market leader.

In 2006, Lexus introduced the RX 400h, the world's first luxury-hybrid SUV powered by gasoline-electric technology. Its 270-horsepower V-6 engine muscles the car from zero to 60 miles per hour in less than eight seconds, while also generating electric power for cruising that makes the RX 400h's fuel efficiency comparable to that of a compact sedan. Fuel efficiency is a powerful TouchPoint for today's environmentally conscious buyers. And as a green bonus, the hybrid's emissions, which are among the lowest in the industry, give it the rating of a Super Ultra Low Emission Vehicle (SULEV). Finally, a guilt-free SUV that also boasts unequaled performance, safety, and luxury features. No wonder the car generated more pre-launch sales volume than any car in the company's history. But even that admirable achievement was not enough for Lexus, a company that clearly has its finger on the pulse of the green movement. At this writing, the company was planning to unveil its first hybrid-only luxury car in January 2009. Patterned after parent Toyota's popular Prius, the newest Lexus model aims to stake a claim as the world's first hybrid luxury car.

As its cars have evolved, so has the Lexus brand. The changes have been subtle, and in harmony with the changes in the market and the Lexus Product TouchPoints. With the introduction of the GS and RX 300, for instance, Lexus modified its slogan, reconfiguring its "relentless" drive for perfection into a "passionate" pursuit. As befits a car company born of a command "to be better than the best," Lexus understands that brand overpromises cannot remain static; they must be constantly managed, evaluated, and adapted to keep step with changes in the marketplace, your company, and the world at large. Lexus's choice of the word "passionate" is a bid to infuse the brand with more emotion, in line with its emphasis on the vehicles' performances and the excitement they ignite. The change indicates to customers that they can now expect even more than they were typically used to from Lexus.

The brand has been enhanced and supported in other ways, too. Early on, as a way to introduce the car to customers, Lexus marketed to rental companies. But in 1995, when the managers decided that fleet sales weren't good for resale values, customer satisfaction, or the basic luxury image, they cut off a source of sales that had grown to ten thousand cars a year. Overall sales volume dropped that year, but so what? Volume, Lexus declared, is not what drives a luxury brand. The sales would come back from sources that were more solid—and so they did.

I've seen other brands make this kind of rolling readjustment, but I've never seen anyone do it better than Lexus.

System TouchPoints, the Lexus Way

From the beginning, Lexus designed its System TouchPoints to make sure customers had a flawless experience every time they interacted with the company, particularly when their cars needed servicing. Lexus's high-end European competitors were especially vulnerable when it came to service; "suffering the badge" often meant chronic breakdowns, long waits for parts, driving rattletrap "loaner" cars, or even having to rent a replacement. Worse yet were cavalier dealers who merely shrugged when customers complained.

To exploit its rivals' weaknesses, Lexus management seized on a superior dealer network that turned out to be the carmaker's most important System TouchPoint. Parent Toyota's reputation for quality drew hundreds of dealer applications when word spread that it was planning a luxury car. Lexus enticed even more dealers by offering unprecedented levels of support.

But to ensure profitability, it limited the number of dealers to fewer than a hundred at the car's launch and about double that figure at full production. Ninety percent came from the top drawer of existing Toyota dealers, and the remainder were seasoned dealers with outstanding reputations at rival brands. All were given tours of the Lexus design and production facilities and indoctrinated in the Lexus philosophy, and all were signatories of the Lexus Covenant.

Mechanics attend a regional facility where they receive intensive instruction regarding the car's innards, and the company picks up the cost of the training. To increase the mechanics' commitment to Lexus and its product line, master certified associates are offered special terms to lease a Lexus for their personal use.

The dealerships themselves have been designed to convey solid luxury and to appeal strongly to the targeted buyers. Inspired by the serenity of Japanese gardens, Toyota designer Jim Sherburne came up with a distinctly untrendy design for a building with a stone facade above a smooth expanse of glass and a stone pillar at each end. To convey integrity and reliability, the look extends to all sides of the building. The Lexus logo is on the left of the facade, and the dealership's name on the right. The size and style of lettering are restricted, and no banners or pennants like those found at many a car dealership are visible. In addition, the stone for the facades comes in three shades of grayish tan: a cool one for conservative locations; a slightly warmer, lighter shade for less formal places; and an even warmer sandy color for Lexus dealerships in the Southwest.

Sherburne's vision extends into the showroom, where coffee tables and leather chairs create a comfortable space for sales representatives to confer with customers. "When you're sitting down around a coffee table, everybody's equal," he explained. Customers waiting for their cars to be serviced do so in lounges specially designed to make them feel like guests in a private home; some even include fireplaces.

No design detail of this System TouchPoint was overlooked. In the service department, for instance, the write-up area is positioned next to the driveway. When a customer drives in, a technician punches the license plate number into a computer and pulls up the car's history as the customer walks through the door to be greeted by name.

Many of these features emanated from an internal research project spearheaded by Dick Chitty, corporate manager for parts and service. Chitty instructed his staff to spend a couple of days writing down every complaint about auto service they had ever heard. The main gripe turned out to be that owners generally have no idea what mechanics do to their cars. More than half of Mercedes owners, Chitty learned, go to independent shops for service—and not because dealer service is too pricey or even because of a lack of convenience. Rather, "they wanted to talk to the person who was going to work on their car," Chitty said. So Lexus converted its senior mechanics into "diagnostic specialists" who wear white shirts and tell customers what's going on. In addition, the service bays are visible from the lounge through a wall of windows so customers can watch their cars being worked on—"like fathers looking in at their newborns," as Sherburne puts it.

But when all is said and done, the dealers have to grasp just one principle, said Dave Illingworth, the Lexus general manager when the brand debuted: "Take care of each customer one at a time." People try to make the auto business very complicated, he said, "but I think, in reality, it's very simple. You just do [that] one thing . . . [and] you'll be just fine."

Of course, the Lexus definition of how to take care of customers goes well beyond the industry standard. For instance, the first two scheduled maintenance visits are free, and any car that comes in for service is washed before it goes back to the owner. If service takes more than a day, the customer gets a loaner car free of charge—and it's a Lexus, not some beat-up compact. The cherry on top of this extraordinary System Touch-Point sundae is a complimentary, twenty-four-hour roadside assistance program that covers a Lexus buyer's costs, if necessary, for a rental car, a hotel room, and up to three days of meals.

It's no wonder that Lexus continues to rack up top ratings in the J.D. Power customer satisfaction surveys. The company has the industry's best dealer-servicing record, with 64 percent of Lexus cars on the road for ten years or less still maintained by Lexus dealers. What is more, this horde of satisfied customers has put Lexus at the top of the industry, along with Toyota, in sales per dealership—not to mention having the industry's happiest and most profitable dealers.

Still, it's not enough. Like any good overpromiser and overde-liverer, Lexus knows it must constantly renew and upgrade its System TouchPoints as its brand evolves and conditions change. To that end, the company regularly sends top executives to meet with dealers to guarantee that their suggestions and complaints are heard. A few years back, a group of Lexus officials set out on a multi-city New Luxury Tour of the United States. They wanted to invite dealers and associates across the country to suggest new and better System TouchPoints. The tour was never intended to bring marching orders to the troops. Instead, the headquarters team wanted to hear people's ideas and tap into solutions that fit their particular operations—even though those solutions might never be adapted for use by dealers in other markets. Lexus values the input of its dealers, and its aim was to build on existing strengths to reach higher levels of excellence.

The effort paid off. The company made a massive investment in a systems upgrade; over a two-year span, Lexus dealers put $500 million into improving their facilities. Individual initiatives arising from the tour have been both bold and creative.

The Carlsbad, California, dealership, for instance, turned its lounge into a virtual home away from home, complete with marble and wood trim, big-screen plasma TVs, and fine artwork. Waiting customers can watch television, admire the art, sip a cappuccino and munch a pastry, or plug into the Internet at any of ten stations. If customers can work productively at the dealership, says general manager Gene Manganiello, they don't have to waste time driving back and forth to the office. It's also just a nice place to spend time. "I overheard one customer telephoning a friend to come join her in our lounge because she was so impressed with the facility," says Manganiello.

One dealer installed a Saks Fifth Avenue boutique and another a full-service spa to align with what has been called "The Lexus Lifestyle." TouchPoints like this have been known to inspire serious discussions between husband and wife about who gets to take the car in for service.

Meanwhile, in the New York City exurbs of northern New Jersey, the New Luxury Tour inspired dealer Ray Catena to revolutionize his entire sales process, streamlining it to eliminate customer pressure and reduce hassle in the dealing. Catena employs several product specialists who are far removed from the stereotypical car salesman—college-educated, salaried professionals who wander around the showroom providing detailed information about the cars and their features and answering the questions of browsing customers. Only when a customer expresses a definite interest in buying does the product specialist introduce him or her to a sales consultant who will write up the deal.

And at Park Place Lexus in Plano, Texas, a committee of a dozen employees called the 50-50 Program is responsible both for spotting problems and finding solutions. The committee has come up with ideas large and small, from reducing waiting time for customer service to offering classes in English as a second language for Spanish-speaking employees to help them develop new skills and earn promotions. "You can truly see the pride and loyalty they have for Park Place," says Wendy Simmons, the dealership's human resources manager, and that, she says, "ultimately translates to our customers." Building on its success, the dealership also started offering courses in Spanish as a second language, on the theory that the classes would facilitate bonding among its employees and help the English speakers better relate to the Spanish-speaking community. Basically, says president Jordan Case, "We're sending the message that we care about our associates"—and that can only help in the endless process of strengthening the Systems TouchPoint for their customers.

The Lexus System TouchPoints are flexible and varied, but they all work to support the brand's prime goal of ensuring a smooth and comfortable experience for the customer.

Human TouchPoint, the Lexus Way

As with most luxury products, the Human TouchPoint is crucial to Lexus's success. Human contact is inevitable in selling and servicing cars, and it has to be pleasant, courteous, attentive, and responsive to a customer's every need if Lexus is to satisfy and retain its targeted buyers. To start customers off with the right impression, the company cues its Human TouchPoint from the top: Many new owners get a personal call from an employee at the company's U.S. headquarters in Torrance, California, welcoming the buyer to the Lexus family and making sure everything about the purchase has been satisfactory. All associates get a calling list of five to ten customers every month, and they receive small incentive rewards for completing their lists. The calling isn't seen as a chore, however, but as a way to connect with customers.

Every Lexus employee who comes into contact with customers—which means just about everyone—is instructed in the precepts of the Lexus Covenant. Sales associates are also required to attend the Lexus Promise class and earn formal certification before they are allowed on the showroom floor. And unlike sales associates at many luxury-car dealers, they are trained to treat every potential customer in a courteous and helpful manner; there is no room for open skepticism about a person's where-withal or a sarcastic attitude intended to make a customer feel grateful just to get a test drive. Instead, Lexus dealers and sales associates welcome potential customers as guests, and they go to great lengths to solve customer problems of every kind.

Indeed, the entire corporate culture is tuned to respond instantly and unhesitatingly to any customer who has a problem, no matter what it may be. Jill Dittrick, an editor at *Lexus Luxury* magazine, recalls the case of a second-time Lexus buyer who was thrilled with everything about her car and delighted with the whole transaction. But having left her favorite cassette tape in her old car, the woman wondered if someone could retrieve it for her. Dittrick immediately called the customer satisfaction group, which in turn called the dealer, whose technicians found the tape and returned it to the customer. The point of the story, Dittrick says, is that it's not unusual. Customers frequently make such requests and "people don't balk" at accommodating them, she said. "They just think, 'Okay, let's see if we can [do] it.'"

TouchPoints Survive the Test

If Lexus is confident and surefooted, it's because, early in its history—in September 1989, to be exact—its TouchPoints survived a challenge that could have spelled disaster. With just eight thousand of the newly introduced LS 400 cars on the road and their buyers having been promised nothing less than perfection, flaws suddenly appeared. First, an owner in Texas discovered defective housing in his center-rear brake light. Then, within a matter of days, the twenty-four-hour roadside-assistance program reported two more problems: a dead battery and a locked-up cruise control system.

What to do? A recall would easily fix model-wide problems—if that's what they were. But the plastic brake-light housing appeared to have gone soft in the Texas sun, the battery died because of a loose alternator connection, and the cruise-control failure stemmed from a supplier's faulty actuator. If these problems had come after years of a good track record, a recall could have been shrugged off. But, as Dave Illingworth remembered, the general question was: "Do we really need to do this? Maybe this was just a one-case thing. Do we dare risk a safety recall on the 'perfect' car under these circumstances?"

It didn't take long to make the decision. "Everybody realized we had to step up and take our licks," said Illingworth. "A lot of people will make fun of us. The competition is going to have a field day with this. But the one thing we will do is take care of the people that bought the car." On December 1, a "special service campaign" was announced. If they manage it right, thought Yuki Togo, Toyota's U.S. division head, "this can make us stronger. It seems like bad luck, but we can turn it into good luck."

But Togo's optimistic outcome seemed unlikely at first, given that such recalls can take a year to complete. Too slow, said Dick Chitty; the service manager wanted this one done before Christmas—in twenty days. Replacement-part production had to be ramped up and a training video prepared for the mechanics. Dealers were encouraged to contact owners personally, before the official letters went out, and elaborate plans were made to service the cars of the many customers who lived more than two hundred miles from their dealers.

"Oh my God, here comes trouble," said a midwestern dealer. Sure enough, the reaction was fierce. "Yes, the Japanese are human too," wrote the *Los Angeles Times. Automotive News* noted dryly that rival luxury-car makers were "amused," and the *Wall Street Journal* warned that the recall was "certain to hurt" the Lexus image.

But Lexus mobilized all its System and Human TouchPoints to deal with the crisis. Engineers were flown in from Japan. Managers in Torrance were sent off to dealerships to lend a hand. Every technician was assigned overtime work for the duration. Dealers hired extra mechanics, kept their service bays open far into the night, and rounded up new cars to use as loaners for customers inconvenienced by the recall. Many owners had their cars picked up and delivered by dealers, who assigned sales personnel as drivers in the emergency. Some customers found a rose on the dashboard when their cars came back.

Owners in remote locations got house calls from technicians who were crisscrossing the country. A mechanic was flown to Alaska to service the state's only Lexus, which luckily was in Anchorage and not in the bush. Technicians did their repairs at a local Toyota dealership if there was one; if not, they rented space at an independent repair shop. Lacking any facility, they fixed the car in the owner's garage or driveway. Their orders were to contact the customer, get the job done the best way they could, get the car washed, and hand it back to the owner with a full tank of gas. If the tank was already full, they were instructed to give the owner a check for a full tank of premium fuel.

The operations manager of the western-area training facility at Irvine, California, spent two crisis weeks on the road. He found one owner hang gliding in the middle of the Mojave Desert. After repairing the guy's car, he couldn't find a car wash—a Lincoln dealer had one, but wouldn't let him use it. So the manager left a $20 bill on the dashboard with a note of apology. Chitty later told him that the owner called to say he'd "never had a rep who fixed his car, filled it with gas, and left money."

In the end, all the repairs were completed by December 20—

and Lexus was, indeed, stronger for the whole incident. What could have been a disaster became a triumph of customer relations, and the month's sales figures actually rose to summer levels. "People could not believe what happened to their neighbors and their friends," says Carl Sewell, a dealer in Texas. "It turned out to be such a positive." *Time* wrote that the recall campaign was a lesson in "Zen and the Art of Automobile Maintenance," and concluded, "Lexus has created virtually instant brand loyalty, a feat unprecedented in the luxury-auto market."

It has been said that perfection is a journey, not a destination. But Lexus is clearly intent on putting the lie to such silly pessimism. The desire to live up to its brand promise and achieve flawless performance at every level of its operation truly inspires this company and its employees. Lexus exemplifies overpromising and overdelivering at its very best.

CHAPTER 9

A Case in Touchpoint: Apple

E very Monday morning like clockwork, in an office building at 1 Infinite Loop, Cupertino, California, Steve Jobs
gathers his top people for a marathon review of the past
week at Apple Inc. They examine sales figures for every product.
They get a status report on every single gadget in development.
They look into the reasons why this or that item is behind in
shipments or experiencing a technical glitch. Jobs has a visceral
distaste for bureaucratic routine in general and meetings in particular, but this one is sacrosanct.

In the winter of 2007, just weeks before Apple was scheduled
to introduce its revolutionary iPhone to the world, Jobs walked
into the Monday morning meeting and announced that he was

not pleased with the enclosure design for the new product. "I can't convince myself to fall in love," he said, "and this is the most important product we've ever done."

As he told *Fortune* magazine, "We pushed the reset button." It meant the iPhone team would have to begin again, poring over earlier models and ideas, hunting for new solutions, all this with the clock ticking double-time. "It was hell," Jobs allowed. The research and design staff labored endless hours under unrelenting pressure, and they succeeded. Jobs declared the new look "dramatically better." The January 2008 introduction went off on time, and the iPhone was a triumph.

There is nothing halfway about Steve Jobs, or about his company's brand overpromise. Apple is all about passion and commitment, but those qualities are directed toward just a few products. "I'm actually as proud of many of the things we haven't done as the things we have done," he says. That's because he understands that spreading a company's passion and commitment and resources across a multitude of products, even good products, inevitably breeds mediocrity. He also has a full measure of courage. The iPod Mini was a huge bestseller, but Apple dropped it the minute Jobs introduced the next-generation iPod, the video-capable Nano.

To overdeliver on an overpromise, you should pay heed to his example. Trying to improve all or even substantial numbers of your TouchPoints isn't necessary—or desirable. Instead, focus on four or five, align them with your overpromise, and push them way out past what the rest of your industry is doing. What you need are extreme, out-of-the-box solutions, not incremental improvements. Find them and I promise your brand will pop.

In this chapter, I describe in some detail how Apple has followed that formula. You will see how it develops its overpromise and then burnishes and aligns carefully chosen Product, System, and Human TouchPoints. First, though, I want to emphasize one key point: Apple does not manage these three TouchPoints as individual, isolated items in the overall brand design ("Today I'll work on my System TouchPoints, tomorrow on my Product TouchPoints") and neither should you. From the start they should be envisioned and crafted as coequal parts of the overdelivery strategy, each reinforcing the others.

You can see Apple deliver on its promise at the Product TouchPoint—in the iPod's incredibly easy to use interface, or the iPhone's weirdly wonderful touch screen. You can see it at the System TouchPoint—in the amazingly inviting and engaging Apple Stores, for example. You can also feel it at the Human TouchPoint—at the Genius Bar where all your iquestions can be answered and your iproblems resolved.

How has this approach worked out for Apple in recent years? Well, between 2002 and 2007, sales tripled to $24 billion, and profits rose almost a hundredfold to $3.5 billion. For those years, Apple led the Fortune 500 with a total return to investors of 94 percent.

Product TouchPoint:
Aligned to Deliver "Insanely Great Design"

The odyssey of Steve Jobs from his founding of Apple in 1976 to his ouster in 1985 to his return in 1997 is too well known to rehash here. Before his so-called wilderness years away from Apple, he had been viewed as an impractical dreamer whose drive for perfection was unconnected to the practical realities of the marketplace. By the time he rejoined the company, he had learned to accommodate his drive for perfection to the bottom line. He quickly slashed costs and shrunk the model line, returning Apple to profitability.

What Jobs could not do was lift Apple's market share much beyond the 4 percent level. The company had committed to a closed-software approach, only to see the Microsoft-Intel pair capture the PC market. Each year saw Jobs bring forth another Macintosh model that was more advanced, user-friendly, elegant (and expensive) than the competition—but to no avail. As superior as Apple was, it could not overcome the realities of the marketplace. It had to move beyond the personal computer to find its salvation.

Over the years, Jobs has settled on the phrase "insanely great products" to describe his vision for Apple. But to my way of thinking, the Apple overpromise is summed up in the emotional comment that people make when they look at an Apple product for the first time. Inevitably, they say, "That's cool!"

What's cool, of course, is not simply the sleek look of the product but the simplicity and elegance with which it opens up a whole new world of fascinating and helpful activities and services. In a word, the design.

In fact, a dedication to superlative design informs every corner of the Apple empire from its offices to its packaging, from its Web site to its products. I would paraphrase Jobs's definition of the company's vision or overpromise as: "We will give you insanely great design."

Along with his commitment to design, Steve Jobs has invested Apple's overpromise with a special emotional intensity and a perfectionist's high expectations. It takes a passionate belief in yourself and your work to cope with all the inevitable hassles and demands on the way to fulfilling those expectations. You have to care about every aspect of the product, down to the tiniest detail.

When the iPod Nano was taking shape, the design called for the front of the case to be white and back panel to be silver. Naturally, there was a seam where the two touched. Jobs would have none of that, and his engineers spent a year figuring out how to eliminate the seam. The result: The Nano is half as thick.

iTunes + iPod = Transformation

The metamorphosis of Apple from an also-ran to a breakaway leader began in 2001 when Steve Jobs, striding around the stage in his customary black shirt and jeans, had the pleasure of introducing four major initiatives (three of them Product TouchPoints): iTunes, the iPod, the OS X computer operating system, and the first Apple Store. It was a tour de force, an almost unimaginable feat that kicked off the company's invasion of the digital media world. OS X made life easier for Macintosh owners, and the Apple Stores would become a major revenue stream. But it was the combination of iTunes and iPod at the Product TouchPoint that would transform Apple's fortunes.

iTunes, of course, was an application that allowed Mac owners to play and organize digital music and, eventually, video files on their computers. They could also use it to manage the music on their iPod. And two years later, with the opening of the iTunes Store online, they could legally and inexpensively download music, music videos, television shows, iPod games, feature-length films, and more. In 2007, the iPhone joined the crowd.

Individually, these products clearly had their attractions, but they were not, on the face of it, unique. There were MP3 players on the scene before the iPod, and some of them had better sound systems. There were smartphones before the iPhone, and they were less expensive and connected to superior networks. As Jobs observes, it doesn't take a soothsayer to spot new waves of technology approaching: "You can see them way before they happen, and you just have to choose wisely which ones you're going to surf."

In each case, Apple surfed into an existing marketplace with a less than perfect product and carved out a sizable chunk for itself. In each case, Steve Jobs succeeded in overdelivering on an overpromise that differentiated Apple from the crowd—and doing so with a compelling Product TouchPoint.

Apple's product development process is not for everyone. It relies on genius, and on a culture that inspires employees to spend virtually every waking hour thinking about how to improve their performance and how to find the next great Apple breakthrough. "We do no market research," Jobs told *Fortune* with evident pride. The iTunes Store, for example, was hatched after he and his aides concluded, "It just seemed like writing on the wall that eventually all music would be distributed electronically."

As for the iPhone: Jobs and his people recognized that they were all unhappy with the software and hardware of their cell phones. "We talked to our friends," he said, "and they all hated their cell phones, too."

Apple may not conduct any formal market research, but you don't have to run focus groups or devise elaborate surveys to find out what kind of products your customers need or want.

Talking to friends is a time-honored way to tap into the public mind. And in this case, it led to the first stage of a Product TouchPoint that aligns with Apple's overpromise: "Let's make a great phone that we can fall in love with."

Before the takeoff of the iPod and iPhone, the company had been treading water with its Macintosh computers, and Jobs and his people were discouraged. "I cannot tell you how important that was to Apple," he says. It reenergized his people, and it showcased the company's engineering and design. A new generation of Macintosh computers was forthcoming that used Intel processors, making it possible to run both Apple and PC applications.

The iPod-loving public took another look at the Macintosh, and suddenly its market share began rising from one quarter to the next. As of the spring of 2008, its share of the U.S. consumer market had soared to 21 percent. And that despite Apple's having bucked the industry downward trend and increased the average price of its computers by more than $150 between 2005 and 2007.

The company's other achievements at the Product Touch-Point have been similarly amazing. As of 2008, the iTunes Store had sold more than five billion songs, and was renting or selling more than fifty thousand movies a day. iPod had a 70 percent market share in the United States and the iPhone was bringing in $4.6 billion, making Apple the third biggest mobile phone maker measured by revenue.

In part, that success has been the result of an intense, company-wide policy of "can you top this?" Steve Jobs's perfectionism demands that Apple researchers and product developers never stop looking for new and better ways of doing things with and to their products. iPods, for example, have evolved from the Mini to the video-enabled Nano to the tiny Shuffle to the mobile-game-friendly Touch—and Apple talks of the next iPod incarnation being the first mainstream Wi-Fi mobile device.

Within a year after the iPhone first appeared, Apple brought forth the iPhone 3G, named in honor of AT&T's third-generation wireless network that enables the new device to download Web pages in less than half the time of the old. Owners can surf and talk simultaneously, and they can hear each other far better with a greatly improved sound system.

The message is clear: No company can afford to rest on its laurels or its Product TouchPoints.

System TouchPoints:
A Portal to Another World

In creating its System TouchPoints—the retail stores and Web site leap to mind—Apple has once again overdelivered on its overpromise of insanely great design. Log onto Apple.com, and the word "cool" leaps from your lips. As for the Apple Stores, they remind me of the philosopher Joseph Campbell's famous analysis of one of the great universal myths, The Hero's Journey. The hero receives a call to adventure and eventually enters through a portal into a strange and magical world where he will overcome challenges, be awarded a great gift, and eventually return through the portal to the ordinary world. When I pass through the portal of an Apple Store, I feel as though I've entered a magical space—a retail venue unlike any other.

Walk into any ordinary electronics store and what do you get? A massed display of gadgets as far as the eye can see, blaring music, harassed salespeople, a bank of cash registers. It's intimidating. Walk into an Apple Store and the atmosphere is like a modern museum—bright, airy, uncluttered, inviting. The products are sitting out on tables and dozens of people of every age and condition are trying them out, having fun with them. You can't resist joining them.

At the System TouchPoint, Apple sucks you in with one non-intimidating experience after another. You start fooling around with the iPod, then a new Mac, then you think you might want to make a movie or create a book—and suddenly you're through another portal into the iLife. Once again, Apple has managed to overdeliver on its overpromise of insanely great design.

Apple.com achieves the same end. The offerings on one of my visits to the home page were fairly typical: a huge, dramatic still-life photo of the iPod Touch ("the funnest iPod ever"), news headlines ("iPhone 3G named gadget of the year"), and photos to take you to various product sites.

There's a rare vividness, freshness, and clarity about these pages. It's no mean trick to package dozens of products, hundreds of applications, and hundreds of film and video offerings in so colorful yet elegant a fashion. Beyond that, you can see the effort that goes into the pages every day to connect the viewer with the world of Apple—the products ("digital camera RAW compatibility update 2.2"), the latest applications ("In turbulent or calm skies, over oceans or mountains," flight simulation via X-Plane 9), the retail stores ("Catch the trailer [for Spike Lee's *Miracle at St. Anna*] on our site, and if you're in New York, hear [him] discuss his new film at the Apple Retail Store SoHo.").

One thing you notice on the Web site as well as in your other encounters with Apple—the company actually supplies you with the words to use when you talk to your friends about your new Apple toy. The MacBook Air is "The world's thinnest notebook," an example of "Thinnovation," while the iPod Shuffle is "The world's most wearable music player." The words are carefully chosen to describe the key selling points of the products. Calling the new iPhone "3G," for example, was a clear message to the technologically literate that this product was going to connect with the Internet far faster and better than its predecessor. The promo is built into the product's name.

Human TouchPoints: A Touch of Genius

Apple's retail stores have been a triumph in terms of differentiating the brand at the Human TouchPoint.

There are two basic levels of employees at the stores. The specialists are the relative newcomers who wander about in their blue T-shirts answering visitors' questions and guiding them around the place. The geniuses are kings. They get to wear a black shirt, à la Steve Jobs, and to sit at the Genius Bar where customers solicit their help with problems. It's a much better gig, with a high paycheck as well as greater status, but geniuses have to demonstrate their full knowledge of essentially everything about everything Mac. Specialists get to be geniuses by studying hard and showing their ability to get along with customers.

It's a great way of inspiring your frontline people to peak performance at the Human TouchPoint.

A friend of mine was among the hundreds of people who stood in line for eight hours in 2007 to buy the first iPhones. When he got to the head of the line, he was handed a sealed bag, which you were not permitted to open in the store. The theory was that it would slow down the whole process because customers would want to know how the iPhone worked and generally occupy the salespeople.

The woman standing in front of my friend had received her bag, all excited, and taken a few steps away from the cash register when she stopped and turned to the clerk. "Can you just answer one question for me?" she asked. She held up the bag. "Can you tell me, what does it do?"

She had waited eight hours in line knowing only that Apple was selling something that had a lot of people intrigued. Sounds crazy, right? But this woman was clearly an Apple customer. She had experienced Apple's overpromises and overdeliveries at the Product, System, and Human TouchPoints, and she was convinced that whatever her company was selling was something she would want to buy.

It was, in my mind at least, the ultimate testimonial. And my friend says she seemed to be pleased when she heard the clerk's answer.

ACKNOWLEDGMENTS

A very special acknowledgment goes to Joel Ehrenpreis, my president of strategic partnership, without whom this book would not have been possible.

This book also would not have been possible without my wife, Keely, who has been a believer and a supporter since its inception.

Thanks also to my mentors and friends, Tony Alessandra, Clay Christianson, Dr. Frank Colleca, Stan Davis, Jim Gilmore, Dr. Peter Kaminski, Ed Keller, John Lee, Stan Leopard, David Morrison, Joe Pine, Adam Slywotski, and Phil Wexler, who have taught me to see the world in new ways.

A special thanks to Bob Kantor for the heads-up on the Blue Man Group; Deanne Ryder, who helped with the initial research and training design; Barbara Saunders, who did exhaustive research to ensure that we had the right agent and publisher; and, of course, my agent Helen Rees. My gratitude also goes to the superb team of writers, editors, and researchers at Wordworks, Inc.—Donna Carpenter, Maurice Coyle, Ruth Hlavacek, Cindy Butler Sammons, Molly Sammons, and Robert W. Stock. And I'd like to thank the publishing team at Portfolio for their work and support of both editions of this book: Adrian Zackheim, Will Weisser, Brooke Carey, Stephanie Land, Christy D'Agostini, and Roland Ottewell.

Thanks, too, to Brad Davis, Craig Davis, Bill Ehrlich, Kerry Killinger, Terry Onustack, Deana Oppenheimer, Sheri Polluck, and Genevieve Smith at WaMu, and to Denny Clements, Jill Dittrick, John Klein, Jason Schultz, Mike Wells, and Perry Wong at Lexus.

I also want to thank Karen Belgard, Frank Bianco, Patti Bianco, Jack Blumenthal, Bob Braddick, Judy Case, Holli Catchpole, Bob Cestaro, Ron Cox, Jim DePolo, Joe DiPasquale, Paul Duffy, Jean English, Korky Kantowski, Bob Lowry, David Perkins, and Dave Zerfoss for their assistance, support, and friendship.

I would also like to acknowledge my clients, who have allowed me to work and learn in their companies.

WORKS CITED

CHAPTER 1:

Overachievers Overpromise

Americangirl.com

"American Girl Sales Up 10 Percent in Second Quarter," *Madison (Wisconsin) Capital Times,* July 22, 2008.

Lisa Bertagnoli, "Girl Power Gives Kick to Tourism," *Crain's Chicago Business,* May 29, 2006.

Ty Burr, "This Girl Has Old-Fashioned Appeal," *Boston Globe,* July 2, 2008.

Emma L. Carew and Susan Feyder, "American Girl Will Doll Up MOA" *(Minneapolis–St. Paul) Star Tribune,* July 8, 2008.

Samantha Critchell, "Girls Identify with American Girl Line, No Matter the Era," *Tulsa World,* July 6, 2008.

Alex Frankel, "Zipcar Makes the Leap," *Fast Company,* March 2008.

Keith H. Hammonds, "American Girl," *Fast Company,* September 2006.

Jane Horwitz, "Kit Kittredge: An American Girl," *Washington Post,* July 4, 2008.

Christopher Palmeri, "What, No Tiny Plastic Hooverville?" *BusinessWeek*, July 7, 2008.

Carla Power, "A Doll That Says It All," *New Statesman*, August 14, 2006.

John Reed, "European Drive for Car-Share Club," *Financial Times*, August 25, 2008.

Ritzcarlton.com

Gail Rosenblum, "Seems Like Old Times" (*Minneapolis–St. Paul*) *Star Tribune*, August 10, 2008.

A. O. Scott, "A Girl's Life," *New York Times*, June 29, 2008.

Michelle Spitzer, "Flood-ravaged Homes Get Cleanup in Melbourne," *Florida Today*, August 24, 2008.

Karen Springen, "Toy Business: American Girl, on the March," *Newsweek*, February 19, 2007.

"Zipcar Low-Car Diet Leads to Permanent Car Loss," *PR Newswire*, August 26, 2008.

"Zipcar Partners with WHERE to Help iPhone Users Hit the Road," *PR Newswire*, July 15, 2008.

"Zipcar Wins Award for Putting Customers at the Center of Its Business Universe," *PR Newswire*, April 18, 2008.

CHAPTER 2:

What's a Brand Overpromise?

Matthew Boyle, "Best Buy's Giant Gamble," *Fortune*, April 3, 2006.

Matthew Boyle, "Brad Anderson," *Fortune*, April 30, 2007.

Frank Burge, "When the Ads Don't Deliver," *EETimes*, November 4, 2002.

Ariana Eunjung Cha, "In Retail, Profiling for Profit," *Washington Post*, August 17, 2005.

Michelle Conlin, "Smashing the Clock," *BusinessWeek*, December 11, 2006.

Diesel.com

"Firestone Settlement Is Approved," *New York Times*, July 5, 2003.

JamesHardie.com

MinuteClinic.com

Mark Scott, "Best Buy Barges into Europe," *BusinessWeek,* May 9, 2008.

Don Tapscott and Anthony D. Williams, "The Wiki Workplace," *Business-Week,* March 26, 2007.

CHAPTER 3:

How Do You Build Your Overpromise?

Yvon Chouinard, "Patagonia: The Next 100 Years," in *Sacred Trusts: Essays on Stewardship and Responsibility,* ed. Michael Katakis (San Francisco: Mercury House, 1993).

Andrew Clark, "Troubled Starbucks Ousts Chief and Pledges Overhaul," *Guardian* (UK), January 2008.

Shireen Dean, "Starbucks Beans Not So Green," *CorpWatch,* March 25, 2002.

Matt Griffin, "A Chat with Paal Gisholt, President/CEO, SmartPak Equine," *Catalog Success,* January 1, 2006.

Patagonia.com

PBTeens.com

Potterybarn.com

Smartpak.com

Craig Vetter, "He's Not Worthy," *Outside,* January 1997.

CHAPTER 4:

How Do You Make
Your Brand Overpromise Unique?

Rick Alden, "How I Did It: Rick Alden, Skullcandy," *Inc.,* September 2008.

"American Ecology," *Seattle Times,* June 8, 2008.

"American Ecology Corp.," *CEO Wire,* March 1, 2007.

"American Ecology Reports Record 2nd Quarter Income," *McClatchy-Tribune Business News,* August 2, 2008.

CardiacScience.com

Cirquedusoleil.com

Commerceonline.com

JCrew.com

Dean Foust, "Hot Growth Companies," *BusinessWeek*, June 9, 2008.

Meryl Gordon, "Mickey Drexler's Redemption," *New York*, November 22, 2004.

Husqvarna.com

"Husqvarna Grows Sales Force," *BNet*, February 2006.

Chris Jones, "Cirque du Soleil and Kooza: Exceeding Expectations," *Chicago Tribune*, June 27, 2008.

Motorcycle.progressive.com

Christopher Palmeri, "American Ecology Is Cleaning Up," *BusinessWeek*, June 9, 2008.

Gordon Pitts, "Daniel Lamarre: Cirque du Soleil," Reportonbusiness.com, August 27, 2007.

Powerheart.com

Progressive.com

Schindler.com

Sherwin-williams.com

Clive Thompson, "Smart Elevators," *New York Times Magazine*, December 10, 2006.

CHAPTER 5:

How Do You Optimize
Your Product Touchpoints?

Richard Jones, "Ahead of the Curve," *Today's Garden Center*, June 2008.

Myyellow.com

Rogersgarden.com

Chuck Salter, "Fresh Start 2002: On the Road Again," *Fast Company*, December 2001.

"The 2007 Medal Awards Takes Center Stage at UC Irvine," *Orange County Business Journal,* September 17–23, 2007.

"Zollars Takes the Helm," *BNet,* December 1999.

CHAPTER 6:

How Do You Optimize
Your System Touchpoints?

Christopher Caggiano, "Building Customer Loyalty, the Harley Way," *Inc.,* November 2000.

Cisco.com

Progressive.com

Chuck Salter, "Progressive Makes Big Claims," *Fast Company,* October 1998.

Stopandshop.com

Sumerset.com

CHAPTER 7:

How Do You Optimize
Your Human Touchpoints?

Jim Abbott, "Then I Saw Blue Man's Bare Faces, Now I'm a Believer," *McClatchy-Tribune Business News,* July 4, 2008.

John Deiner, "On NYC's Streets, A Rhapsody in Blue," *Washington Post,* January 27, 2008.

1800bepetty.com

Ray George, "Brand Tales: How Stories Help Employees Deliver the Brand Promise," Brandchannel.com, March 10, 2008.

Samuel Greengard, "Optimas Update: The Best Get Better," *Workforce,* March 2003.

Jennifer Koch Laabs, "Thinking Outside the Box at The Container Store— Human Resource Management Awards," *Workforce,* March 2001.

Peggy Morrow, "Setting and Measuring Service Standards," *Inc.,* August 2000.

Nordstrom.com

Thecontainerstore.com

VCSFL.com

Rob Walker, "Brand Blue," *Fortune Small Business,* March 2003.

"What's Behind All That Blue?" McClatchy-Tribune News Service, June 5, 2008.

CHAPTER 8:

A Case in Touchpoint: Lexus

Chester Dawson, *Lexus: The Relentless Pursuit* (Hoboken, NJ: John Wiley and Sons, 2004).

S. C. Gwynne, Seiichi Kanise, and Adam Zagorin, "New Kid on the Dock," *Time,* September 17, 1990.

Booyeon Lee, "Lexus Airs Plans for an Eatery, Fountains," *San Diego Union-Tribune,* July 20, 2006.

Lexus.com

Lexus Magazine Online.

CHAPTER 9:

A Case in Touchpoint: Apple

Apple.com

Peter Elkind, "The Trouble with Steve," *Fortune,* March 17, 2008.

Alex Frankel, "Magic Shop," *Fast Company,* November 2007.

Arik Hesseldahl, "The iPhone 3G Unveiled," *BusinessWeek,* June 10, 2008.

James Ledbetter and Jacob Weisberg, "Four Captivating Companies and What They Share," *Washington Post,* September 14, 2008.

Betsy Morris, "What Makes Apple Golden," *Fortune,* March 17, 2008.

Adam L. Penenberg, "All Eyes on Apple," *Fast Company,* December 2007.

Brent Schlender, "The iPhone on Training Wheels," *Fortune,* November 26, 2007.

Matt Vella, "How Great Design Makes People Love Your Company," *BusinessWeek,* September 4, 2008.

David Zeiter, "Apple a Day: Apple Earnings Call Features Steve Jobs, Outstanding Numbers," *The Baltimore Sun,* October 22, 2008.

INDEX